The

ITALIAN
VEGETARIAN

The
ITALIAN
VEGETARIAN

*Fresh, tasty recipes for
healthy eating*

Consulting Editor:
Gabriella Rossi

LORENZ BOOKS

First published in 1999 by Lorenz Books

© Anness Publishing Limited 1999

Lorenz Books is an imprint of
Anness Publishing Limited
Hermes House
88–89 Blackfriars Road
London SE1 8HA

ISBN 0 7548 0072 5

A CIP catalogue record for this book is available from the British Library.

Publisher: Joanna Lorenz
Project Editor: Sarah Duffin; *Designer:* Joyce Chester
Editorial Reader: Hayley Kerr; *Production Controller:* Mark Fennell
Recipes: Angela Boggiano, Carla Capalbo, Jacqueline Clark, Maxine Clark,
Roz Denny, Nicola Diggins, Matthew Drennan, Sarah Edmonds,
Joanna Farrow, Sarah Gates, Shirley Gill, Christine Ingram, Sue Maggs,
Annie Nichols, Stephen Wheeler, Kate Whiteman, Jeni Wright
Photography: William Adams-Lingwood, Karl Adamson,
Edward Allwright, Steve Baxter, James Duncan, Michelle Garrett,
John Heseltine, Amanda Heywood, William Lingwood,
Patrick McLeavey, Michael Michaels, Thomas Odulate, Peter Reilly
Food for photography: Carla Capalbo, Jacqueline Clark, Sarah Edmonds,
Joanna Farrow, Carole Handslip, Wendy Lee, Lucy McKelvie,
Jenny Shapter, Jane Stevenson, Stephen Wheeler
Stylists: Madeleine Brehaut, Hilary Guy, Jo Harris, Clare Hunt,
Blake Minton, Marion Price

Printed and bound in Hong Kong/China

For all recipes, quantities are given in both metric and imperial measures
and, where appropriate, measures are also given in standard cups and
spoons. Follow one set, but not a mixture, because they are not
interchangeable.

1 3 5 7 9 10 8 6 4 2

CONTENTS

Introduction	**6**
Basic Techniques and Recipes	**14**
STARTERS AND SOUPS	**22**
PASTA	**32**
PIZZAS	**54**
RISOTTOS, GNOCCHI AND FRITTATA	**60**
VEGETABLES AND SALADS	**68**
DESSERTS	**84**
BREADS	**90**
Index	**96**

INTRODUCTION

There's no better country for a vegetarian to visit than Italy, whether the journey is an actual trip through its varied and beautiful landscape, or a virtual visit via its cuisine. Italian market stalls are stacked with glorious, glossy vegetables, from the broad beans, spinach and fennel of the north to the sun-kissed tomatoes, aubergines and peppers of the south. This is the nation that put pasta, pizzas and polenta on the menu; the home of ravishing risottos and superb salads. Add a wonderful array of cheeses, succulent olives and the twin delights of basil and balsamic vinegar and it is easy to see why Italian food fits so neatly – and so satisfyingly – into a vegetarian diet.

Italians value their vegetables, often serving them solo as starters (antipasti) or as a simple course to follow pasta. Roasted peppers, tossed with black olives and herbs and baked with a breadcrumb topping, are just too delicious to adulterate. Italians serve them with crusty bread and a few tossed leaves, and savour every mouthful.

Pasta seems too humdrum a word to describe the amazing range of shapes, fresh and dried, plain or coloured, flavoured or filled, that Italian cooks create from the simple amalgamation of flour, salt, water and eggs or oil. Fresh pasta, at one time on sale only at specialist delicatessens, is now stocked by supermarkets, with new varieties available almost daily.

More and more cooks have started making their own pasta, too, either by hand or using one of several machines on the market. If you do make your own pasta – and you'll find full instructions in this book – do experiment with recipes like Coriander Ravioli with Pumpkin Filling, or the equally delicious Tagliatelle with Avocado Sauce. For the vegetarian, pasta presents plenty of options. It can be served very simply, with oil and garlic; can form the basis of a tasty lasagne with mushrooms, or can be dressed up for a formal dinner.

In the north of Italy, where rice replaces pasta as a staple food, risotto rules. This is another wonderful gift for the vegetarian cook. The main ingredient you need for a perfect risotto is patience. Stand dreamily at the cooker, stirring the rice while you gradually add stock, and you will be rewarded with tender, creamy grains and a fabulous flavour. One of the most delicious risottos is a combination of pumpkin and pistachio nuts.

Fruit always forms part of an Italian meal. A bowl of polished apples or perfect peaches might be put on the table at the end of dinner, perhaps with a chunk of Parmesan so meltingly delicious that you will wonder why you only ever used it for cooking before. When desserts are served, they tend to be creamy concoctions or the pastries for which Italian cooks are deservedly famous. Lemon Ricotta Cake, Pine Nut Tart and Lovers' Knots are all delicious, and favourites like Tiramisu and Zabaglione are renowned the world over.

Store Cupboard Ingredients

Pack your pantry or store cupboard with these basic ingredients, and you'll always be able to produce an Italian meal within moments.

Amaretti biscuits
The basis of several Italian desserts, these are also served with sweet wine, for dipping.

Balsamic vinegar
Aged slowly in wooden barrels, the finest varieties are deliciously mellow and fragrant. The taste is quite sweet and concentrated, so only a small quantity is needed.

Capers
Aromatic buds pickled in jars of wine vinegar. Rinse before use.

Dried chillies
These are used in spicy sauces and casseroles. Reconstitute them in water unless you are adding them to a moist dish that will be cooked for a long time.

Olive oil
This is possibly the single most important ingredient in the Italian kitchen. Use extra virgin olive oil in salad dressings and for finishing dishes – its incomparable flavour is marred by high heat. For frying, experiment with several olive oils to find one which has a flavour that you like. Choose the best quality you can afford.

Olives
Italy produces some of the finest olives in the world. Green olives are sharper and crunchier than the black varieties. Use them on their own for antipasti or for sharpening sauces and salads. Buy them loose, if possible, so you can taste them before you take them away.

Olive paste
Available in jars. Olives are pounded to a paste with salt and olive oil. The paste tends to be rich and salty so a little goes far. Delicious on small pieces of toasted crusty bread (*crostini*).

Passata
Puréed and sieved tomato pulp, passata comes in bottles, jars and cartons, and is invaluable for adding to sauces, soups and vegetable dishes.

Pasta
Dried pasta keeps well and is a boon to the busy cook. In addition to long shapes like spaghetti and tagliatelle, stockpile short shapes like penne, farfalle (bows) and conchiglie (shells). Look for the words "durum wheat" on the packet, as this is top quality pasta which produces good results. Some vegetarians prefer wholewheat pasta, which has a nuttier taste and slightly chewier texture.

Essential store cupboard ingredients include olives and nuts.

Pine nuts
These come from the cones of the stone pine. They are very popular throughout the Mediterranean countries, and are an essential ingredient in pesto. Pine nuts can be used in both sweet and savoury dishes, and are often fried in butter and sprinkled with salt as a snack to serve with drinks.

Pistachio nuts
Popular in Italy since the sixteenth century, these are used in both sweet and savoury dishes. Try them in a pumpkin risotto.

Polenta
The coarsely-ground yellow maize is a staple of the northern Italian diet. It can be either eaten hot or left to cool and set, in which case it is usually brushed with oil and grilled before being served.

Porcini mushrooms
These mushrooms, also known as Boletus or ceps, are found in the woods in various parts of Europe. In late summer and early autumn, some are used fresh, while the surplus is sun-dried to provide flavour for the rest of the year. Dried porcini mushrooms are expensive, but a few go a long way. Reconstitute in warm water then chop them before use.

Pulses
A typical Italian store cupboard will always contain a supply of these highly nutritious ingredients. The most popular pulses include the pretty red and cream speckled borlotti beans, the small white cannellini beans and the larger black-eyed beans.

Chick-peas, known as *ceci* in Italy, are also popular, as are dried broad beans (*fave*). Italian lentils are grown in the area around Umbria. Small and brown, they do not break up during cooking.

Rice
Particularly popular in northern Italy, rice is the basic ingredient in risotto. Of the special short-grain varieties grown for this purpose, the best known are *arborio*, *vialone nano* and *carnaroli*.

Saffron
Although the most expensive spice, only a few threads add a piquant flavour and rich golden colour to risottos and sauces.

Sun-dried tomatoes
The plain dried tomatoes are sold in packets and must be reconstituted before use. Also available are jars of sun-dried tomatoes in olive oil. The flavoured oil can be used in cooking and salad dressings.

Sunflower oil
A useful all-round oil, this is ideal for deep-fried dishes. Some cooks like to use a mixture of sunflower oil and olive oil for cooking delicately flavoured foods.

Too good to hide: display these colourful ingredients, but keep them out of direct sunlight. From left, they are sunflower oil, sun-dried tomato paste, extra virgin olive oil, passata and pure olive oil. After opening, containers of passata must be kept in the fridge.

Fresh Produce

Vegetables, fruit and herbs play a vital role in all Italian cooking, which is good news for vegetarians. Italians insist on really fresh produce, often visiting the market twice a day. Follow their example and buy only the freshest possible fruit and vegetables, preferably locally or organically-grown. If you live in the country, buy from farm stalls or, better still, pick your own. It is worth investigating box schemes: local suppliers deliver boxes or seasonal organic produce to your door.

Vegetables and Fruit

Italians enjoy a wide range of vegetables and fruit. From the temperate north come green beans, broad beans, broccoli, cabbage, leeks, carrots and both cultivated and wild mushrooms. Apples and pears are popular, along with berry fruits in season. As you travel south, peaches and citrus fruits appear, the tomatoes ripen more rapidly and Mediterranean vegetables like courgettes, aubergines and peppers are piled high on market stalls. Italians are not as fond of potatoes as some of their neighbours are, but when they do cook them, they are delicious. Potatoes are used to make gnocchi, and baked potatoes layered with tomatoes is a popular dish. Italian roast potatoes are very good, thanks largely to being cooked in butter (north) or oil (south). An intriguing alternative to green asparagus, a white variety is found in north-eastern Italy. It is grown under mounds of soil to ensure that the spears are not touched by the sun. Both varieties can be boiled or roasted in olive oil and served with butter and freshly grated Parmesan cheese. Among the many different leaves used in salads, radicchio and rocket are particularly popular. Fennel is used fresh in salads and is also baked as a vegetable dish. Globe artichokes are found throughout Italy. They are a type of thistle, which explains their bulbous appearance. Quarter small tender bulbs and braise with olive oil, parsley and garlic.

Herbs

Basil is probably the most well known Italian herb. Famously used in pesto, basil is also added to many different soups and pasta dishes as it complements tomatoes perfectly. Grow your own basil, if you can, and tear the leaves instead of chopping them. Italians favour flat leaf parsley, and are also fond of marjoram, oregano, thyme, sage and rosemary. Some recipes include dried herbs, but fresh herbs are generally preferred.

Right, clockwise from top left: *Peaches, pears, apples and raspberries, sweetcorn, peppers, fresh herbs, carrots, vine and beefsteak tomatoes, potatoes, leeks, mushrooms and courgettes, broccoli and cabbage. In the trug are green beans, broad beans and peas.*

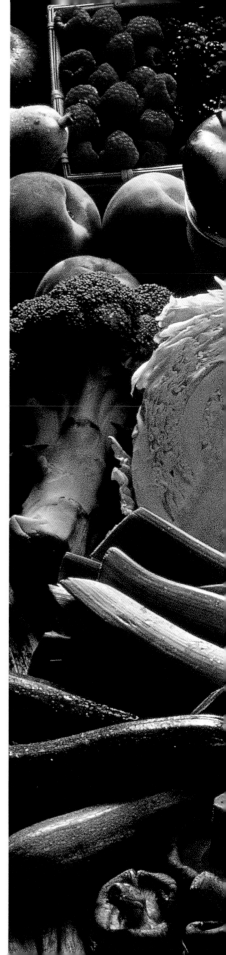

Equipment

Many of the utensils in the Italian kitchen are everyday items found in most kitchens, but some specialized ones are particularly useful. Pasta can be made by hand, but a pasta machine will make it much lighter work, and trying to serve spaghetti from the pan without a special spoon is very frustrating. If you are serving pizzas, a cutting wheel will cut them into clean slices.

Biscuit cutter
Usually used for cutting biscuit dough but is equally good for cutting fresh pasta shapes.

Colander
Indispensable for draining hot pasta and vegetables.

Earthenware pot
Excellent for slow-cooking stews, soups or sauces. It can be used either in the oven or on top of the stove on a gentle heat with a metal heat diffuser under it to prevent cracking. Many shapes and sizes are available. To season a terracotta pot before using it for the first time, immerse it in cold water overnight. After removing, fill with water and bring slowly to the boil. Discard the water. Repeat the process, changing the water, until the "earth" taste disappears.

Fluted pastry cutter
For cutting fresh pasta or pastry.

Hand food mill
Excellent for soups, sauces and tomato "passata": the pulp passes through the holes, leaving the seeds and skin behind.

Ice cream scoop
Better than an Italian scoop for firm and well-frozen ice creams.

Icing nozzles
For piping decorations, garnishes, etc. Use with a nylon or paper pastry bag.

Italian ice cream scoop
Good for soft ices that are not too solid.

Mallet
A mallet is a very useful implement to have in a vegetarian kitchen. It can be used for crushing nuts and whole spices.

Olive stoner
Can be used for removing the stones from olives or cherries.

Palette knife
Very useful for spreading and smoothing.

Parmesan cheese knife
In Italy, Parmesan is not cut with a conventional knife, but broken off the large cheese wheels using this kind of wedge. Insert the point of the knife and apply firm pressure.

Pasta machine
Many models are available, including sophisticated electric and industrial models. Most have an adjustable roller width and thin and wide noodle cutters.

Pasta rolling pin
A length of dowelling 5 cm/2 in in diameter can also be used. Smooth the surface of the wood with fine sandpaper before using for the first time.

Pestle and mortar
For hand-grinding spices, rock salt, peppercorns, herbs and breadcrumbs.

Pizza cutting wheel
Useful for cutting slices, although a sharp knife may also be used.

Spaghetti spoon
The wooden "teeth" catch the spaghetti strands as they boil.

Whisk
Excellent for smoothing sauces and beating egg whites.

Wide vegetable peeler
Very easy to use for peeling all sizes of vegetable.

Basic Techniques and Recipes

Processing Pasta Dough

1 Assemble the ingredients for a basic pasta dough (see page 19). Sift the flour into the bowl and add a grinding of salt.

2 Pour in the beaten eggs and oil and chosen flavouring, if using, and process until the dough begins to come together. Tip out the dough and knead until smooth. Wrap the dough and leave to rest for 30 minutes. Use as required.

Using a Pasta Machine

1 Feed the rested dough several times through the highest setting first, then reduce the settings until the required thickness is achieved.

2 A special cutter will produce fettuccine or tagliatelle. A narrower cutter will produce spaghetti or tagliarini.

To Cook Pasta

1 Tip the pasta into a large pan of boiling salted water. Stir once to prevent sticking. The addition of 15 ml/1 tbsp vegetable or olive oil will help to stop the water boiling over and prevent the pasta from sticking. *Do not cover* or the water will boil over.

2 Quickly bring the pasta back to a rolling boil and boil until *al dente* (literally "to the tooth") – the pasta should be just firm to the bite. It should neither have a hard centre nor be soft.

3 Drain the pasta well, using a large colander or sieve. Immediately rinse the pasta with boiling water to wash off any starch and to prevent the pasta from sticking together. At this stage you can toss the pasta in a little olive oil or butter if not dressing with the sauce immediately. Serve hot pasta straight away. It is up to you whether you toss the pasta with the sauce before serving or serve it with the sauce on the top.

Cooking Times for Fresh and Dried Pasta

Calculate the cooking time from the moment the water returns to the boil after the pasta has been added. The timings given are only suggested as a guide: check the instructions on the packet as pasta varies according to the manufacturer. There are also several quick-cooking varieties on the market.

Unfilled pasta
Fresh: 2–3 minutes, though some very thin pasta is ready as soon as the water returns to the boil. The pasta will be ready when it rises to the surface of the water.
Dried: 8–12 minutes, but check often.

Filled pasta
Fresh: 8–10 minutes.
Dried: 15–20 minutes.

Chopping an Onion

Chopped onions are used in many Italian vegetarian recipes and, whether they are finely or roughly chopped, the method is the same; just vary the gap between cuts.

1 Cut off the stalk end of the onion and cut it in half through the root, leaving the root intact. Remove the skin and place the halved onion, cut-side down, on the board. Make lengthways vertical cuts into the onion, taking care not to cut right through to the root.

2 Make two or three horizontal cuts from the stalk end through to the root, but without cutting all the way through.

3 Cut the onion across from the stalk end to the root. The onion will fall away in small squares. Cut further apart for larger squares.

Peeling Tomatoes

If you have the time, peel tomatoes before adding them to sauces or cooked dishes. This avoids those unwanted, rolled-up, tough pieces of tomato skin that can spoil a dish.

1 Make a cross in each tomato with a sharp knife and place in a heatproof bowl.

2 Pour over enough boiling water to cover and leave to stand for 30 seconds. The skins should start to come away. The skins of slightly unripe tomatoes may take a little longer.

3 Drain the tomatoes and peel the skin away with a sharp knife. Don't leave the tomatoes in the boiling water for too long as they tend to soften.

Preparing Chillies

Chillies add a distinct flavour to vegetarian dishes, but you may wish to remove the seeds.

1 Always protect your hands, as chillies can irritate the skin; wear rubber gloves and never rub your eyes after handling chillies. Halve the chilli lengthways and remove and discard the seeds, if you like.

2 Slice, chop finely and use as required. Wash the knife and board thoroughly in hot, soapy water. Always wash your hands thoroughly after preparing chillies.

Chopping Herbs

Chop herbs just before you use them; the flavour will then be much fresher.

1 Remove the leaves and place on a clean dry board. Use a large, sharp cook's knife (a blunt knife will bruise, not chop, the herbs).

2 Chop the herbs, as finely or as coarsely as required, by holding the tip of the blade on the board and rocking the handle up and down.

Preparing Garlic

Don't worry if you don't have a garlic press: try this method, which gives wonderful juicy results.

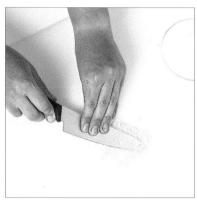

1 Break off the clove of garlic, place the flat side of a large knife on top and strike with your fist. Remove all the papery outer skin. Begin by finely chopping the clove.

2 Sprinkle over a little table salt and, using the flat side of a large knife blade, work the salt into the garlic, until the clove softens and releases its juices. Use as required.

Thinly Slicing Vegetables

Some of the recipes call for thinly sliced vegetables; without a food processor, this could be quite tricky, but not with this technique.

1 Peel the vegetables as required. Take a thin slice off one side, to give a solid base to stand on. This will prevent the vegetable from sliding around.

2 Stand the vegetable on its flat base and then thinly slice with a sharp knife. Use your knuckles as a guide and try to keep your fingers tucked underneath.

Stoning Olives

Using a stoner is the easiest way to remove the stone from an olive, but you can also use a sharp knife to cut out the stone.

1 Put the olive in the stoner, pointed end uppermost.

2 Squeeze the handles together to extract the stone.

Flavoured Oils

For extra flavour brush these over the pizza base before adding the topping. The oils also form a kind of protective seal that keeps the base crisp and dry on the outside.

CHILLI OIL
INGREDIENTS
150 ml/¼ pint/⅔ cup olive oil
10 ml/2 tsp tomato purée
15 ml/1 tbsp dried red chilli flakes

1 Heat the oil in a pan until very hot but not smoking. Stir in the tomato purée and red chilli flakes. Leave to cool.

2 Pour the chilli oil into a small jar or bottle. Cover and store in the fridge for up to 2 months (the longer you keep it the hotter it will get).

GARLIC OIL
INGREDIENTS
3–4 whole garlic cloves
120 ml/4 fl oz/½ cup olive oil

1 Peel the garlic cloves and put them into a small jar or bottle.

2 Pour in the oil, cover and keep in the fridge for up to 1 month.

Basic Pizza Dough

This simple bread base is rolled out thinly for a traditional pizza recipe.

Makes one of the following:

1 × 25-30 cm/10-12 in round pizza base

4 × 13 cm/5 in round pizza bases

1 × 30 × 18 cm/ 12 × 7 in oblong pizza base

INGREDIENTS
175 g/6 oz/1½ cups strong white
  flour
1.5 ml/¼ tsp salt
5 ml/1 tsp easy-blend dried yeast
120-150 ml/4-5 fl oz/½-⅔ cup
  lukewarm water
15 ml/1 tbsp olive oil

1 Sift the flour and salt into a large mixing bowl.

2 Stir in the yeast.

3 Make a well in the centre of the dry ingredients. Pour in the water and oil and mix with a spoon to a soft dough.

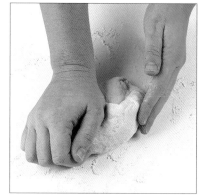

4 Knead the dough on a lightly floured surface for about 10 minutes until smooth and elastic.

5 Place the dough in a greased bowl and cover with clear film. Leave in a warm place to rise for about 1 hour or until the dough has doubled in bulk.

6 Knock back the dough. Turn on to a lightly floured surface and knead again for 2–3 minutes. Roll out as required and place on a greased baking sheet. Push up the edge to make a rim. The dough is now ready for topping.

Basic Pasta Dough

Serves 3-4

INGREDIENTS
200 g/7 oz/1³/₄ cups plain white flour
a pinch of salt
2 large eggs, beaten
15 ml/1 tbsp olive oil

I Sift the flour and salt on to a clean work surface and make a well in the centre with your fist.

2 Pour the beaten eggs and oil into the well. Gradually mix in the eggs with your fingers.

3 Knead the pasta until smooth, wrap and allow to rest for at least 30 minutes before attempting to roll out. The pasta will be much more elastic after resting.

Vegetable Stock

Makes about 1.5 litres/
2½ pints/6¼ cups

INGREDIENTS
1 onion
2 carrots
2 large celery sticks, plus any small
    amounts of the following: leeks,
    celeriac, parsnip, turnip, cabbage
    or cauliflower trimmings,
    mushroom peelings
30 ml/2 tbsp vegetable oil
bouquet garni
6 black peppercorns
1.75 litres/3 pints/7½ cups water

I Peel, halve and slice the onion. Roughly chop the remaining vegetables.

2 Heat the oil in a large pan and fry all the vegetables until soft and lightly browned. Add the bouquet garni and peppercorns and pour in the water.

3 Bring to the boil, skim the surface then lower the heat, partially cover the pan and simmer for 1½ hours. Strain the stock and allow to cool. Store in the fridge for 2–3 days.

Pesto

Pesto is a delicious sauce which can be used on its own or stirred into soured cream or mayonnaise to use as a quick dip. Use a good quality olive oil.

Makes about 300 ml/½ pint/1¼ cups

INGREDIENTS
50 g/2 oz/about 2 cups fresh basil
   leaves
1–2 garlic cloves
45 ml/3 tbsp freshly grated Parmesan
   cheese
45 ml/3 tbsp pine nuts, lightly toasted
60–90 ml/4–6 tbsp virgin olive oil,
   plus extra for sealing
salt and freshly ground black pepper

1 Put the basil leaves, garlic, Parmesan cheese and pine nuts in a food processor. Season with salt and pepper and process until well blended, scraping down the side of the bowl once or twice to ensure even mixing.

2 With the machine running, gradually pour the oil through the feeder tube until a smooth paste forms. Pour the pesto into a jar and spoon over a little more oil to seal the surface. Cover tightly and keep in the fridge for up to one week, or freeze in smaller quantities.

Easy Tomato Sauce

This sauce can be used as the base for pasta or vegetable sauces, as a pizza base or a seasoned dip. Use ripe tomatoes and your favourite herbs.

Makes about 325 ml/11 fl oz/1⅓ cups

INGREDIENTS
30 ml/2 tbsp olive oil
1 large onion, chopped
1–2 garlic cloves, chopped
2.5 ml/½ tsp chopped fresh thyme
   leaves or 1.5 ml/¼ tsp dried thyme
1–2 bay leaves
6–8 ripe plum tomatoes, chopped
60 ml/4 tbsp water or stock
5–10 ml/1–2 tsp chopped
   fresh herbs

1 In a large frying pan heat the oil over a medium heat. Add the onion and cook until softened. Add the garlic, thyme and bay leaves and cook for 1 minute more. Stir in the tomatoes and water or stock. Bring to the boil and cook gently, uncovered, for 15–20 minutes until most of the liquid has evaporated and the sauce has thickened.

2 For a chunky sauce, simply remove the bay leaf and stir in the chopped herbs. To make a smooth sauce, purée in a food processor until smooth. Press through a sieve to remove any skin and pips, then stir in the herbs. Cool and keep in the fridge for up to four days.

Béchamel Sauce

The creamy mellowness of a perfect béchamel sauce makes it ideal for vegetarian lasagne as well as a base for many other vegetable dishes.

Serves 4

INGREDIENTS
1 small onion
1 small carrot
1 celery stick
300 ml/½ pint/1¼ cups milk
1 bouquet garni
6 black peppercorns
pinch of freshly grated nutmeg or
    blade of mace
25 g/1 oz/2 tbsp butter
25 g/1 oz/¼ cup plain flour
30 ml/2 tbsp single cream
salt and freshly ground black pepper

1 Chop all the vegetables finely and put them in a saucepan. Pour the milk into the pan.

2 Add the bouquet garni, peppercorns and nutmeg or mace. Bring to the boil. Remove from the heat, cover and allow the milk to infuse for 30 minutes.

3 Melt the butter in a saucepan, remove from the heat and stir in the flour. Return to the heat and cook the roux for 1–2 minutes.

4 Reheat the flavoured milk to almost boiling. Strain into a heatproof jug, pressing the vegetables with the back of a spoon to extract the juices.

5 Off the heat, gradually stir the milk into the roux, stirring vigorously after each addition.

6 Bring to the boil and stir continuously until the sauce thickens. Simmer gently for 3–4 minutes. Remove from the heat, adjust the seasoning to taste and stir in the cream.

COOK'S TIP
Flaked almonds or crisply fried buttered crumbs can be sprinkled over the sauce before serving for an added crunch.

Pepper Gratin

Serve this simple but delicious starter with a small mixed leaf or rocket salad and some good crusty bread to mop up the juices from the peppers.

Serves 4

INGREDIENTS
2 red peppers
30 ml/2 tbsp extra virgin olive oil
60 ml/4 tbsp fresh white
   breadcrumbs
1 garlic clove, finely chopped
5 ml/1 tsp drained bottled capers
8 stoned black olives, roughly
   chopped
15 ml/1 tbsp chopped fresh oregano
15 ml/1 tbsp chopped fresh flat leaf
   parsley
salt and freshly ground black pepper
fresh herbs, to garnish

red peppers

olive oil

fresh breadcrumbs

garlic

parsley

black olives

oregano

capers

COOK'S TIP
Don't skin the grilled peppers under the running tap as the water could wash away some of the delicious smoky flavour.

1 Preheat the oven to 200°C/400°F/Gas 6. Place the peppers under a hot grill. Turn occasionally until they are blackened and blistered all over. Remove from the heat and place in a plastic bag. Seal and leave to cool.

2 When cool, peel the peppers. Cut them in half and remove the seeds, then cut the flesh into large strips.

3 Use a little of the olive oil to grease a small baking dish. Arrange the pepper strips in the dish.

4 Scatter the rest of the ingredients on top, drizzle with the remaining olive oil and add salt and pepper to taste. Bake for about 20 minutes until the breadcrumbs have browned. Garnish with the fresh herbs and serve straight away.

Sweet and Sour Artichoke Salad with Salsa

The sweet and sour sauce that works so well in this salad is called *agrodolce* in Italy, where it is often served with artichokes.

Serves 4

INGREDIENTS
6 small globe artichokes
juice of 1 lemon
30 ml/2 tbsp olive oil
2 medium onions, roughly chopped
175 g/6 oz/1½ cups shelled fresh or
    thawed frozen broad beans
300 ml/½ pint/1¼ cups boiling water
175 g/6 oz/1½ cups fresh or frozen
    peas
salt and freshly ground black pepper
fresh mint leaves, to garnish

FOR THE SALSA AGRODOLCE
120 ml/4 fl oz/½ cup white wine
    vinegar
15 ml/1 tbsp caster sugar
handful of fresh mint leaves, roughly
    torn

globe artichokes

lemon juice

olive oil

onions

white wine vinegar

caster sugar

mint

peas

broad beans

1 Peel the outer leaves from the artichokes and discard. Cut the artichokes into quarters and place in a bowl of water and the lemon juice.

2 Heat the oil in a large saucepan. Add the onions and fry for about 10 minutes, until golden. Add the beans and stir, then drain the artichokes and add them to the pan. Pour in the water and cook, covered, for 10–15 minutes.

3 Add the peas, season with salt and pepper and cook for 5 minutes more, stirring from time to time, until the vegetables are tender. Strain the vegetables, tip them in a bowl, leave to cool, then cover and chill.

4 To make the salsa agrodolce, mix all the ingredients in a small pan. Heat gently for 2–3 minutes until the sugar has dissolved. Simmer gently for about 5 minutes, stirring occasionally. Leave to cool. To serve, drizzle the salsa over the vegetables and garnish with the extra mint leaves.

Dolcelatte-stuffed Pears

These pears, with their scrumptious creamy topping, make a sublime dish when served with a simple salad.

Serves 4

INGREDIENTS

50 g/2 oz/¼ cup ricotta cheese
50 g/2 oz dolcelatte cheese, rind removed
15 ml/1 tbsp clear honey
½ celery stick, finely sliced
8 stoned green olives, roughly chopped
4 dates, stoned and cut into thin strips
pinch of paprika
4 ripe pears
150 ml/¼ pint/⅔ cup apple juice

honey

ricotta cheese

pears

dates

dolcelatte cheese

green olives

celery

apple juice

1 Preheat the oven to 200°C/400°F/ Gas 6. To make the filling, place the ricotta in a bowl and crumble in the dolcelatte. Add the rest of the ingredients except for the pears and apple juice. Mix well and set aside.

2 Halve the pears lengthwise and use a melon baller to remove the cores. Place in a baking dish and divide the filling equally among them.

3 Pour in the apple juice and cover the dish with foil. Bake for 20 minutes or until the pears are tender. Remove the foil and place the dish under a hot grill for 3 minutes. Serve immediately.

COOK'S TIP
Choose ripe pears in season such as conference, Williams' or Comice.

Tricolore Pasta Salad with Pine Nuts

A salad made from ingredients representing the colours of the Italian flag makes a good talking point. Try to use buffalo mozzarella cheese.

Serves 4

INGREDIENTS
175 g/6 oz/1½ cups farfalle (pasta bows)
1 large ripe avocado
6 ripe red tomatoes
225 g/8 oz mozzarella cheese
30 ml/2 tbsp pine nuts, toasted
1 fresh basil sprig, to garnish

FOR THE DRESSING
90 ml/6 tbsp olive oil
30 ml/2 tbsp red wine vinegar
5 ml/1 tsp balsamic vinegar (optional)
5 ml/1 tsp wholegrain mustard
pinch of sugar
salt and freshly ground black pepper
30 ml/2 tbsp chopped fresh basil

1 Cook the pasta in plenty of boiling salted water following the instructions on the packet. Drain well and cool.

olive oil   avocado   basil   pine nuts   tomatoes   mozzarella cheese   wholegrain mustard   pasta bows   red wine vinegar

2 Halve the avocado, remove the stone and peel off the skin. Slice the flesh lengthways. Slice the tomatoes and mozzarella cheese into thin rounds.

3 Arrange the tomato, mozzarella cheese and avocado in overlapping slices around the edge of a flat plate. Whisk all the dressing ingredients together in a small bowl.

4 Toss the pasta with half the dressing and the chopped basil. Pile into the centre of the plate. Pour over the remaining dressing, scatter over the pine nuts and garnish with a fresh basil sprig. Serve immediately.

Minestrone

This has to be one of the world's greatest soups, a glorious combination of pasta, beans and fresh vegetables cooked in a herby tomato sauce.

Serves 4

INGREDIENTS
45 ml/3 tbsp olive oil
1 large leek, thinly sliced
2 carrots, chopped
1 courgette, thinly sliced
115 g/4 oz whole green beans, halved
2 celery sticks, thinly sliced
1.5 litres/2½ pints/6¼ cups vegetable
    stock or water
400 g/14 oz can chopped tomatoes
15 ml/1 tbsp chopped fresh basil
5 ml/1 tsp chopped fresh thyme
    leaves or 2.5 ml/½ tsp dried thyme
400 g/14 oz can cannellini or kidney
    beans
50 g/2 oz/½ cup macaroni or small
    pasta shapes
salt and freshly ground black pepper
freshly grated Parmesan cheese and
    chopped fresh parsley, to garnish

1 Heat the olive oil in a large saucepan, add all the fresh vegetables and heat until sizzling. Cover the pan, lower the heat and sweat the vegetables for 15 minutes, shaking the pan from time to time.

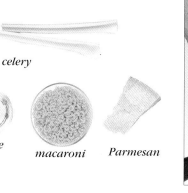

leek
carrots
green beans
courgette
chopped tomatoes
cannellini beans
basil

celery
olive oil
macaroni
Parmesan

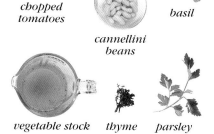

vegetable stock   *thyme*   *parsley*

COOK'S TIP

Like gazpacho, minestrone made solely from vegetables is delicious served cold on a hot summer's day. In fact the flavour improves if the soup is made a day or two ahead and stored in the fridge. It can also be frozen and reheated.

2 Pour in the stock or water and add the tomatoes and herbs with salt and pepper to taste. Bring to the boil, replace the lid, then simmer gently for about 30 minutes.

3 Add the beans with the can liquid, then tip in the pasta. Simmer for a further 10 minutes. Check the seasoning and serve hot sprinkled with the Parmesan cheese and parsley.

Tuscan Bean Soup

There are lots of versions of this wonderful soup. This one uses cannellini beans, leeks, cabbage and good olive oil – and tastes even better reheated.

Serves 4

INGREDIENTS
60 ml/4 tbsp virgin olive oil
1 onion, roughly chopped
2 leeks, roughly chopped
1 large potato, diced
2 garlic cloves, finely chopped
1.2 litres/2 pints/5 cups vegetable stock
400 g/14 oz can cannellini beans, drained, liquid reserved
175 g/6 oz Savoy cabbage, shredded
45 ml/3 tbsp chopped fresh flat leaf parsley
30 ml/2 tbsp chopped fresh oregano
75 g/3 oz Parmesan cheese, shaved
salt and freshly ground black pepper

FOR THE GARLIC TOASTS
30–45 ml/2–3 tbsp virgin olive oil
6 thick slices country bread
1 garlic clove, bruised

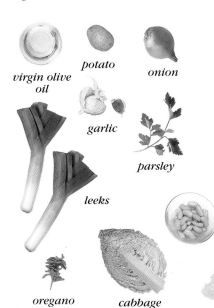

virgin olive oil   *potato*   *onion*   *garlic*   *parsley*   *leeks*   *oregano*   *cabbage*   *cannellini beans*   *Parmesan cheese*   *country bread*   *vegetable stock*

1 Heat three-quarters of the oil in a large pan and gently cook the onion, leeks, potato and garlic for 4–5 minutes.

2 Pour in the stock and the reserved liquid from the beans. Cover and simmer for 15 minutes.

3 Stir in the cabbage and beans, with half the herbs. Season and cook for 10 minutes more. Spoon about one-third of the soup into a food processor or blender and process until fairly smooth. Return the blended portion to the soup in the pan, taste for seasoning and heat through for 5 minutes.

4 Meanwhile make the garlic toasts. Drizzle a little oil over the slices of bread, then rub both sides of each slice with the garlic. Toast until browned on both sides. Ladle the soup into bowls. Sprinkle with the remaining herbs and the Parmesan shavings. Drizzle with the remaining oil and serve with the toasts.

Creamy Parmesan and Cauliflower Soup with Pasta Bows

A silky smooth, mildly cheesy soup which isn't overpowered by the cauliflower.

Serves 6

INGREDIENTS
1 large cauliflower
1.2 litres/2 pints/5 cups vegetable
    stock
175 g/6 oz/1½ cups pasta bows
    (farfalle)
150 ml/¼ pint/⅔ cup single cream
freshly grated nutmeg
pinch of cayenne pepper
60 ml/4 tbsp freshly grated Parmesan
    cheese
salt and freshly ground black pepper

MELBA TOAST
3–4 slices day-old white bread
freshly grated Parmesan cheese, for
    sprinkling
1.5 ml/¼ tsp paprika

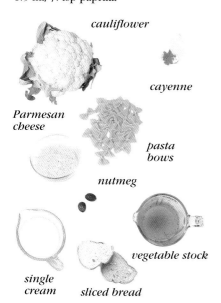

cauliflower

cayenne

Parmesan
cheese

pasta
bows

nutmeg

vegetable stock

single
cream

sliced bread

1 Cut the leaves and central stalk away from the cauliflower and discard. Divide the cauliflower into florets.

2 Bring the stock to the boil and add the cauliflower. Simmer for about 10 minutes or until very soft. Remove the cauliflower with a slotted spoon and place in a food processor.

3 Add the pasta to the stock and simmer for 10 minutes until tender. Drain, reserving the pasta, and add the liquid to the food processor with the cream, nutmeg and cayenne. Blend until smooth, then press through a sieve into a clean pan. Stir in the cooked pasta. Reheat the soup, stirring occasionally. Stir in the Parmesan. Taste and adjust the seasoning.

4 Meanwhile make the melba toast. Preheat the oven to 180°C/350°F/ Gas 4. Toast the bread lightly on both sides. Quickly cut off the crusts and split each slice in half horizontally. Scrape off any doughy bits and sprinkle the toast with Parmesan cheese and paprika. Place on a baking sheet and bake in the oven for 10–15 minutes or until uniformly golden. Serve with the soup.

Fresh Tomato Soup

Flavoursome sun-ripened tomatoes need little embellishment in this fresh-tasting soup. It is sensational hot, but just as delicious chilled.

Serves 6

INGREDIENTS

1.5 kg/3-3½ lb ripe tomatoes
400 ml/14 fl oz/1⅔ cups vegetable
    stock
45 ml/3 tbsp sun-dried tomato paste
30–45 ml/2–3 tbsp balsamic vinegar
10–15 ml/2–3 tsp caster sugar
small handful of fresh basil leaves,
    plus extra, to garnish
salt and freshly ground black pepper

TO SERVE
sliced ciabatta
Parmesan cheese
double cream

tomatoes

vegetable
stock

sun-dried
tomato paste

caster
sugar

double
cream

balsamic
vinegar

Parmesan
cheese

basil

ciabatta

COOK'S TIP

If you buy the tomatoes from the supermarket, choose ripe vine tomatoes and add sugar and vinegar as necessary, depending on their natural sweetness.

1 Plunge the tomatoes into boiling water for 30 seconds, then refresh in cold water. Peel away the skins and quarter the tomatoes.

2 Put the tomatoes in a large saucepan and pour over the stock. Bring just to the boil, reduce the heat, cover and simmer gently for 10 minutes until the tomatoes are pulpy.

3 Stir in the sun-dried tomato paste, vinegar, sugar and basil. Season, then cook gently, stirring, for 2 minutes. Process the soup in a blender or food processor, then press through a sieve into a clean pan. Reheat gently.

4 Meanwhile, grate the Parmesan cheese and pile it on top of the ciabatta slices. Grill until the cheese melts and turns golden. Serve the soup in warmed bowls, with one or two cheese croûtons on top of each portion. Add a spoonful of cream and garnish with basil.

Egg and Cheese Soup

In this classic Roman soup, eggs and cheese are beaten into hot stock, producing a slightly curdled texture characteristic of the dish.

Serves 6

INGREDIENTS
3 eggs
45 ml/3 tbsp fine semolina
90 ml/6 tbsp Parmesan cheese,
    freshly grated
1.5 litres/2½ pints/6¼ cups vegetable
    stock
salt and freshly ground black pepper
12 rounds of crusty bread, to serve
pinch of nutmeg

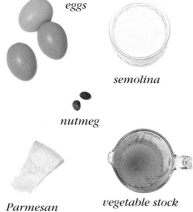

eggs

semolina

nutmeg

Parmesan cheese

vegetable stock

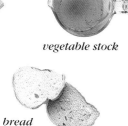

bread

1 Beat the eggs in a bowl with the semolina and the Parmesan cheese, then add the nutmeg. Take 1 cupful of the stock. Do not heat this, it must be cool when added. Beat it into the eggs, adding only a little at a time.

2 Meanwhile heat the remaining stock to simmering point in a large saucepan.

3 A few minutes before you are ready to serve the soup, whisk in the egg mixture. Raise the heat slightly until the soup is barely boiling. Season with salt and pepper. Cook for 3–4 minutes. As the egg cooks, the soup will look slightly curdled.

4 To serve, toast the rounds of crusty bread and place 2 in the bottom of each soup plate. Ladle on the hot soup, and serve immediately.

Leek, Potato and Rocket Soup

The distinctive, peppery taste of rocket is wonderful in this filling and satisfying soup. Serve it hot with ciabatta croûtons.

Serves 4-6

INGREDIENTS

50 g/2 oz/¼ cup butter
1 onion, chopped
3 leeks, chopped
2 potatoes, diced
900 ml/1½ pints/3¾ cups vegetable
   stock or water
2 large handfuls rocket, roughly
   chopped
150 ml/¼ pint/⅔ cup double cream
salt and freshly ground black pepper
garlic-flavoured ciabatta croûtons,
   to serve

butter   *onion*

double cream

rocket

leeks

vegetable stock

potatoes

COOK'S TIP

To make the croûtons, cut ciabatta into cubes and fry in a mixture of olive oil and butter until crisp. Flavour the oil with garlic, if you like.

1 Melt the butter in a large heavy-based pan, add the onion, leeks and potatoes and stir until the vegetables are coated in butter.

2 Cover and leave the vegetables to sweat for about 15 minutes. Pour in the stock, cover again, then simmer for about 20 minutes more, until the vegetables are tender.

3 Press the soup through a sieve or food mill and return to the clean pan. When puréeing the soup, don't use a blender or food processor, as either of these would give the soup a gluey texture. Add the chopped rocket and cook gently for 5 minutes.

4 Stir in the cream, then season to taste and reheat gently. Ladle the soup into warmed soup bowls, then serve with a few garlic-flavoured ciabatta croûtons in each.

Spaghetti with Fresh Tomato Sauce

The heat from the pasta will release the delicious flavours of this sauce. Only use the really red and soft tomatoes – large ripe beefsteak or Marmande tomatoes are ideal. Don't be tempted to use small hard tomatoes: they are much less juicy.

Serves 4

INGREDIENTS
4 large ripe tomatoes
2 garlic cloves, finely chopped
60 ml/4 tbsp chopped fresh herbs
    such as basil, marjoram, oregano
    or flat leaf parsley
150 ml/¼ pint/⅔ cup olive oil
salt and freshly ground black pepper
450 g/1 lb spaghetti

chopped
fresh
herbs

olive oil

spaghetti   garlic

tomatoes

1 Plunge the tomatoes into a saucepan of boiling water for 30 seconds – no longer or they will become mushy.

2 Lift out with a slotted spoon and plunge into a bowl of cold water. Peel off the skins, then dry the tomatoes on kitchen paper.

3 Halve the tomatoes and squeeze out the seeds. Chop into small cubes and mix with the garlic, herbs, olive oil and seasoning in a non-metallic bowl. Cover and allow the flavours to blend for at least 30 minutes.

4 Cook the pasta in plenty of boiling salted water, following the instructions on the packet.

5 Drain the pasta and return it to the clean pan. Add the sauce and toss to mix. Cover with a lid and leave for 2 minutes, then toss again and serve straight away.

VARIATION
Mix 115 g/4 oz/⅔ cup stoned and chopped black olives into the sauce just before serving.

Spaghetti with Mixed Bean Chilli Sauce

Warm up those winter nights with this hearty bean mixture matched with pasta.

Serves 6

INGREDIENTS

1 onion, finely chopped

1–2 garlic cloves, crushed

1 large fresh green chilli, seeded and chopped

150 ml/¼ pint/⅔ cup vegetable stock

400 g/14 oz can chopped tomatoes

30 ml/2 tbsp concentrated tomato purée

120 ml/4 fl oz/½ cup red wine

5 ml/1 tsp dried oregano

200 g/7 oz French beans, sliced

400 g/14 oz can red kidney beans, drained

400 g/14 oz can cannellini beans, drained

400 g/14 oz can chick-peas, drained

450 g/1 lb spaghetti

salt and freshly ground black pepper

onion

spaghetti

green chilli

garlic

French beans

chick-peas

red kidney beans

cannellini beans

oregano

vegetable stock

red wine

tomato purée

chopped tomatoes

1 To make the sauce, put the chopped onion, garlic and chilli into a pan with the stock. Bring to the boil and cook for 5 minutes.

2 Add the tomatoes, tomato purée, wine and oregano, with salt and pepper to taste. Stir well. Bring the mixture to the boil, cover, lower the heat and simmer the sauce for 20 minutes.

3 Cook the French beans in a pan of boiling salted water for about 5–6 minutes until just tender. Drain the beans thoroughly.

4 Stir all the beans and the chick-peas into the sauce. Simmer for a further 10 minutes. Meanwhile, cook the spaghetti in boiling, salted water, following the instructions on the packet. Drain thoroughly, transfer to a serving dish and top with the chilli beans.

Spaghetti with Mushroom and Olive Sauce

Sweet cherry tomatoes provide the perfect foil to the rich, pungent sauce that coats the pasta in this delicious supper dish.

Serves 4

INGREDIENTS
15 ml/1 tbsp olive oil
1 garlic clove, chopped
225 g/8 oz/3 cups mushrooms, chopped
150 g/5 oz/scant 1 cup stoned black olives
30 ml/2 tbsp chopped fresh parsley
1 fresh red chilli, seeded and chopped
450 g/1 lb spaghetti
225 g/8 oz cherry tomatoes
slivers of Parmesan cheese, to serve (optional)

garlic

mushrooms

fresh red chillies

cherry tomatoes

black olives

spaghetti

parsley

olive oil

1 Heat the oil in a large pan. Add the garlic and cook for 1 minute. Add the mushrooms, cover, and cook over a medium heat for 5 minutes.

2 Tip the mushroom mixture into a blender or food processor and add the olives, parsley and red chilli. Blend until smooth.

COOK'S TIP
Italian cooks favour flat leaf parsley.

3 Cook the pasta in boiling salted water following the instructions on the packet. Drain well and return to the pan. Add the olive mixture and toss together until the pasta is well coated. Cover and keep warm.

4 Heat an ungreased frying pan and shake the cherry tomatoes around for 2–3 minutes or until they start to split. Serve the pasta topped with the tomatoes. Garnish with slivers of Parmesan, if you like.

Tagliatelle with Double Tomato Sauce

Sun-dried tomatoes add pungency to this dish, while the grilled fresh tomatoes give it a lovely juicy flavour.

Serves 4

INGREDIENTS
45 ml/3 tbsp olive oil
1 garlic clove, crushed
1 small onion, chopped
50 ml/2 fl oz/¼ cup dry white wine
6 drained sun-dried tomatoes in oil, chopped
30 ml/2 tbsp chopped fresh flat leaf parsley
50 g/2 oz/⅓ cup stoned black olives, halved
450 g/1 lb fresh tagliatelle
4 tomatoes, halved
Parmesan cheese, to serve
salt and freshly ground black pepper

tomatoes

parsley

garlic

onion

sun-dried tomatoes

tagliatelle

black olives

dry white wine

Parmesan cheese

olive oil

1 Heat 30 ml/2 tbsp of the oil in a pan. Add the garlic and onion and cook for 2–3 minutes. Add the wine, sun-dried tomatoes and parsley. Cook for 2 minutes. Stir in the black olives.

2 Bring a large pan of salted water to the boil. Add the fresh tagliatelle and cook for 2–3 minutes until just tender.

3 Put the tomatoes on a tray and brush with the remaining oil. Grill for 3–4 minutes.

4 Drain the pasta, return it to the pan and toss with the sauce. Serve with the grilled tomatoes, freshly ground black pepper and shavings of Parmesan cheese.

Tortellini with Three Cheeses

Serve this straight from the oven while the cheese is still runny. If smoked mozzarella cheese is not available, try using a smoked German cheese or even grated smoked Cheddar.

Serves 4-6

INGREDIENTS
450 g/1 lb/4 cups fresh tortellini
2 eggs
350 g/12 oz/1½ cups ricotta cheese
25 g/1 oz/2 tbsp butter
25 g/1 oz/⅔ cup fresh basil leaves
115 g/4 oz/1 cup smoked cheese, such as mozzarella or Cheddar, grated
60 ml/4 tbsp freshly grated Parmesan cheese
salt and freshly ground black pepper

smoked cheese

tortellini

basil

eggs

butter

Parmesan cheese

ricotta cheese

1 Preheat the oven to 190°C/375°F/Gas 5. Cook the tortellini in plenty of boiling salted water, following the instructions on the packet. Drain well.

2 Beat the eggs with the ricotta cheese and season well with salt and pepper. Use the butter to grease an ovenproof dish. Spoon in half the tortellini, pour over half the ricotta mixture and cover with half the basil.

3 Cover with the smoked cheese and remaining basil. Top with the rest of the tortellini and spread over the remaining ricotta mixture.

4 Sprinkle Parmesan cheese evenly over the top. Bake for 35–45 minutes or until the cheese topping is golden-brown and bubbling.

Tagliatelle with an Avocado Sauce

The combination of pale green tagliatelle and a velvety avocado sauce looks elegant and tastes superb. The sauce is rather rich, so you don't need too much of it.

Serves 6

INGREDIENTS

3 ripe tomatoes
2 large ripe avocados
25 g/1 oz/2 tbsp butter, plus extra for tossing the pasta
1 garlic clove, crushed
350 ml/12 fl oz/1½ cups double cream
dash of Tabasco sauce
450 g/1 lb green tagliatelle
freshly grated Parmesan cheese
60 ml/4 tbsp soured cream
salt and freshly ground black pepper

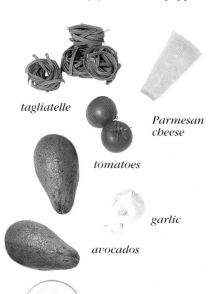

tagliatelle

Parmesan cheese

tomatoes

garlic

avocados

soured cream

double cream

butter

1 Cut the tomatoes in half and remove the cores. Squeeze out the seeds and dice the flesh. Set aside.

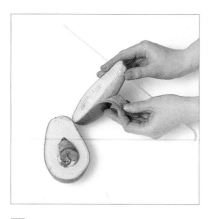

2 Cut the avocados in half, take out the stones and remove the peel. Roughly chop the flesh.

3 Melt the butter in a saucepan and add the garlic. Cook over a low heat for 1 minute, then add the cream and chopped avocados. Raise the heat, stirring constantly to break up the pieces of avocado.

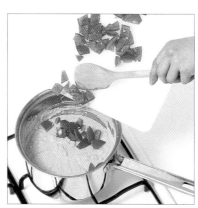

4 Add the diced tomatoes and season to taste with salt, pepper and a little Tabasco sauce. Keep warm.

5 Cook the pasta in boiling salted water, following the instructions on the packet. Drain well, return to the clean pan and toss with a knob of butter.

6 Divide the pasta among four warmed bowls and spoon over the sauce. Sprinkle with grated Parmesan cheese and top each portion with a spoonful of soured cream.

Penne with Aubergine and Mint Pesto

This splendid variation on the classic Italian pesto uses fresh mint and walnuts rather than basil and pine nuts for a different flavour.

Serves 4

INGREDIENTS
2 large aubergines
450 g/1 lb/4 cups dried penne
50 g/2 oz/¹/₂ cup walnut halves

FOR THE PESTO
25 g/1 oz/²/₃ cup fresh mint
15 g/¹/₂ oz/3 tbsp flat leaf parsley
40 g/1¹/₂ oz/scant ¹/₂ cup walnuts
40 g/1¹/₂ oz/¹/₂ cup freshly grated
    Parmesan cheese
2 garlic cloves
90 ml/6 tbsp olive oil
salt and freshly ground black pepper

penne
garlic
olive oil
walnuts
parsley
Parmesan cheese
mint
aubergines

1 Cut the aubergines lengthwise into 1 cm/¹/₂ in slices.

2 Cut the slices again crossways to give short strips.

3 Layer the strips in a colander with salt and leave to stand for 30 minutes over a plate to catch any juices. Rinse well in cool water and drain.

4 Place all the pesto ingredients, except the oil, in a blender or food processor, blend until smooth, then gradually add the oil in a thin, steady stream until the mixture amalgamates. Season to taste.

5 Cook the penne in boiling salted water, following the instructions on the packet. When the pasta is nearly cooked, after about 8 minutes, add the aubergine and cook for 3 minutes more.

6 Drain well and tip into a bowl. Toss with the mint pesto and walnut halves. Serve immediately.

Lemon and Parmesan Capellini with Herb Bread

Cream flavoured with Parmesan cheese and lemon makes a superb sauce for pasta.

Serves 2

INGREDIENTS
½ Granary baguette
50 g/2 oz/¼ cup butter, softened
1 garlic clove, crushed
30 ml/2 tbsp chopped fresh herbs
225 g/8 oz dried or fresh capellini
250 ml/8 fl oz/1 cup single cream
75 g/3 oz/1 cup freshly grated
    Parmesan cheese
finely grated rind of 1 lemon
salt and freshly ground black pepper
chopped fresh flat leaf parsley, and
    lemon rind, to garnish

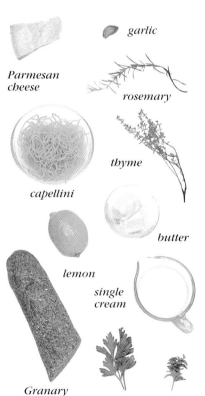

garlic

Parmesan
cheese

rosemary

thyme

capellini

butter

lemon

single
cream

Granary
baguette   parsley   oregano

1 Preheat the oven to 200°C/400°F/ Gas 6. Holding a sharp knife at an angle, cut the baguette into thick slices.

2 Put the butter in a bowl and beat in the garlic and herbs. Spread thickly over each slice of bread.

3 Reassemble the baguette. Wrap in foil, support on a baking sheet and bake for 10 minutes.

4 Meanwhile, bring a large pan of water to the boil and cook the pasta until just tender. Dried pasta will take 10–12 minutes, fresh pasta will be ready in 2–3 minutes.

5 Pour the cream into another pan and bring to the boil. Stir in the Parmesan and lemon rind. The sauce should thicken in about 30 seconds.

6 Drain the pasta, return it to the pan and toss with the sauce. Season to taste and sprinkle with a little chopped fresh parsley and grated lemon rind, if you like. Serve with the hot herb bread.

Pasta with Gorgonzola and Walnut Sauce

This is a very quick but indulgently creamy sauce. Serve the pasta with a green salad for a delicious lunch or supper.

Serves 2

INGREDIENTS

50 g/2 oz/¼ cup butter
50 g/2 oz/½ cup button mushrooms, sliced
150 g/5 oz Gorgonzola cheese
150 ml/¼ pint/⅔ cup soured cream
115 g/4 oz/1 cup dried pasta shapes, such as farfalle or penne
25 g/1 oz/¼ cup Pecorino cheese, grated
50 g/2 oz/½ cup broken walnut pieces
salt and freshly ground black pepper

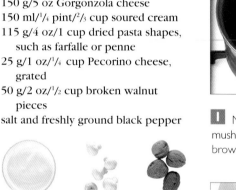

soured cream   *button mushrooms*   *walnuts*

butter

Pecorino cheese   *Gorgonzola cheese*

COOK'S TIP

Gorgonzola is probably one of Italy's best known cheeses, an honour it shares with Parmesan. Like all blue cheeses, Gorgonzola is best when freshly cut from the whole cheese. Avoid cheese that shows signs of sweating.

1 Melt the butter and fry the sliced mushrooms over a low heat until lightly browned and softened.

2 With a fork, mash the Gorgonzola with the soured cream. Add salt and pepper to taste. Cook the pasta in boiling salted water, following the instructions on the packet.

3 When the pasta is almost ready, stir the Gorgonzola cream into the mushroom mixture and heat gently until the cheese has melted.

4 Finally stir in the Pecorino cheese and the walnut pieces. Drain the pasta, tip it into a warmed bowl and toss with the sauce. Serve immediately.

Farfalle with Mushrooms and Cheese

Fresh wild mushrooms are very good in this sauce, but they are expensive. To cut the cost, use a mixture of wild and cultivated mushrooms.

Serves 4

INGREDIENTS

15 g/¹/₂ oz/1 cup dried porcini
    mushrooms
250 ml/8 fl oz/1 cup warm water
1 onion
25 g/1 oz/2 tbsp butter
1 garlic clove, crushed
225 g/8 oz/scant 3 cups fresh
    mushrooms, thinly sliced
a few fresh sage leaves, very finely
    chopped, plus a few whole leaves,
    to garnish
150 ml/¹/₄ pint/²/₃ cup dry white wine
225 g/8 oz/2 cups dried farfalle (pasta
    bows)
115 g/4 oz/¹/₂ cup mascarpone cheese
115 g/4 oz Gorgonzola or torta di
    Gorgonzola cheese, crumbled
salt and freshly ground black pepper

butter

farfalle

Gorgonzola

white wine

onion

fresh mushrooms

garlic

mascarpone cheese

dried mushrooms

sage

1 Soak the dried porcini in the water for 20–30 minutes. Lift out of the liquid and squeeze hard. Strain and reserve the liquid. Finely chop the porcini.

2 Chop the onion finely and fry with the porcini in the butter in a large pan, for 3 minutes. Add the garlic, fresh mushrooms, chopped sage and seasoning. Cook, stirring frequently, for 5 minutes until the mushrooms are soft. Stir in the soaking liquid and the wine and simmer.

3 Cook the farfalle in a large pan of boiling salted water, following the directions on the packet.

VARIATION
For a lighter sauce, use Greek-style yogurt instead of mascarpone.

4 Meanwhile, stir the mascarpone and Gorgonzola cheeses into the mushroom sauce. Heat through, stirring, until melted. Taste for seasoning. Drain the pasta thoroughly, add to the sauce and toss to mix. Serve at once, with black pepper ground liberally on top. Garnish with sage leaves.

Spinach and Ricotta Conchiglie

Italians use large pasta shells to hold a variety of delicious stuffings. Few are more pleasing than this mixture of chopped spinach and ricotta cheese.

Serves 4

INGREDIENTS

350 g/12 oz large conchiglie
450 ml/³/₄ pint/1³/₄ cups passata or
   tomato pulp
275 g/10 oz frozen chopped spinach,
   thawed
50 g/2 oz crustless white bread,
   crumbled
120 ml/4 fl oz/¹/₂ cup milk
60 ml/4 tbsp olive oil
225 g/8 oz/2 cups ricotta cheese
pinch of grated nutmeg
1 garlic clove, crushed
2.5 ml/¹/₂ tsp black olive paste
25 g/1 oz/¹/₃ cup freshly grated
   Parmesan cheese
25 g/1 oz/¹/₃ cup pine nuts
salt and freshly ground black pepper

black
olive paste

pine
nuts

Parmesan
cheese

garlic

white
bread

spinach

olive
oil

milk

ricotta
cheese

conchiglie

passata

1 Cook the pasta in boiling salted water, following the directions on the packet. Drain, refresh under cold water, drain again and reserve until needed.

2 Pour the passata or tomato pulp into a nylon sieve over a bowl and strain to thicken. Place the spinach in another sieve and press out any excess liquid with the back of a spoon.

3 Place the bread and milk in a food processor. Add 45 ml/3 tbsp of the oil and process briefly to combine. Add the spinach and ricotta cheese and season with salt, pepper and nutmeg. Process briefly to mix evenly.

4 Combine the passata with the garlic, remaining olive oil and black olive paste. Spread the sauce evenly over the bottom of an ovenproof dish. Preheat the oven to 180°C/350°F/Gas 4.

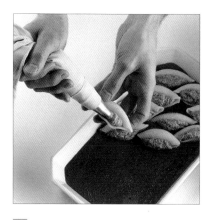

5 Spoon the spinach mixture into a piping bag fitted with a large plain nozzle and fill the pasta shapes (alternatively fill with a spoon). Arrange the pasta shapes over the sauce. Cover with foil.

6 Bake for 20 minutes, or until the pasta is hot. Remove the foil, scatter with Parmesan cheese and pine nuts, and return the bake to the oven for 5–10 minutes to brown the cheese.

Coriander Ravioli with Pumpkin Filling

A stunning herb pasta with a superb creamy pumpkin and roast garlic filling.

Serves 4-6

INGREDIENTS
200 g/7 oz/1¾ cups strong
   unbleached white flour
2 eggs
pinch of salt
45 ml/3 tbsp chopped fresh
   coriander, plus coriander sprigs,
   to garnish

FOR THE FILLING
4 garlic cloves in their skins
450 g/1 lb pumpkin, peeled, cubed
   and seeds removed
115 g/4 oz/½ cup ricotta cheese
4 halves drained sun-dried tomatoes
   in olive oil, finely chopped, plus
   30 ml/2 tbsp oil from the jar
freshly ground black pepper

coriander

pumpkin   *eggs*

garlic

flour

ricotta cheese

sun-dried tomatoes

1 Place the flour, eggs, salt and coriander in a food processor. Pulse until combined. Preheat the oven to 200°C/400°F/Gas 6.

2 Place the dough on a lightly floured board and knead well for 5 minutes, until smooth. Wrap in clear film and leave to rest in the fridge for 20 minutes. Bake the garlic cloves for 10 minutes until softened, then peel.

3 Steam the pumpkin for 5–8 minutes until tender. Mash with the garlic, ricotta and sun-dried tomatoes. Season with black pepper.

4 Divide the pasta into 4 pieces and flatten slightly. Using a pasta machine, on its thinnest setting, roll out each piece. Leave the sheets of pasta on a clean dish towel until slightly dried.

5 Using a 7.5 cm/3 in crinkle-edged round cutter, stamp out 36 rounds.

6 Top half the rounds with mixture. Brush the edges with water and place another round of pasta on top of each. Press the edges firmly to seal. Cook in boiling salted water for 3–4 minutes. Drain well and toss with the sun-dried tomato oil. Garnish with coriander sprigs.

Baked Vegetable Lasagne

Italian cooks really value their vegetables, and often combine sun-ripened tomatoes and mushrooms in a variation on the classic lasagne.

Serves 8

INGREDIENTS
30 ml/2 tbsp olive oil
1 onion, very finely chopped
500 g/1¼ lb tomatoes, fresh or
    canned, chopped
675 g/1½ lb/6 cups cultivated or wild
    mushrooms, or a combination
75 g/3 oz/6 tbsp butter
2 garlic cloves, finely chopped
juice of ½ lemon
400 g/14 oz no-pre-cook lasagne
175 g/6 oz/1½ cups freshly grated
    Parmesan or Cheddar cheese, or a
    combination
salt and freshly ground black pepper

FOR THE BÉCHAMEL SAUCE
750 ml/1¼ pints/3 cups milk
1 bay leaf
3 blades of mace
115 g/4 oz/½ cup butter
75 g/3 oz/⅔ cup plain flour

olive oil
onion
mushrooms
butter
chopped tomatoes
mace
milk
garlic
flour
lemon juice
grated cheese
lasagne
bay leaf

1 Preheat the oven to 200°C/400°F/Gas 6. Heat the oil in a small frying pan and sauté the onion until translucent. Add the chopped tomatoes and cook for 6–8 minutes, stirring often. Season with salt and pepper, and set aside.

2 Make the béchamel sauce. Heat the milk with the bay leaf and mace. In a separate pan, melt the butter, then stir in the flour and cook for 2 minutes. Strain in the hot milk, whisking all the time, until the sauce boils and thickens. Season and set aside.

3 Slice the mushrooms finely. Heat half the butter and cook the mushrooms until the juices flow. Add the garlic and lemon juice, and season with salt and pepper. Cook until the liquid has almost all evaporated and the mushrooms are starting to brown. Set aside.

4 Grease a baking dish with the remaining butter. Spread a large spoonful of the béchamel sauce over the bottom. Arrange a layer of pasta in the dish. Cover the pasta with a thin layer of mushrooms, then one of béchamel sauce. Sprinkle evenly with a little cheese.

5 Make another layer of pasta. Spread with a thin layer of the tomato mixture, and then one of béchamel sauce. Sprinkle with cheese. Repeat the layers, ending with pasta coated with béchamel sauce. Sprinkle with cheese. Bake for around 20 minutes until browned.

Vegetarian Cannelloni

Try this deliciously satisfying alternative to the usual spinach and ricotta cheese cannelloni.

Serves 4-6

INGREDIENTS
1 onion, finely chopped
2 garlic cloves, crushed
2 carrots, coarsely grated
2 celery sticks, finely chopped
150 ml/$^1/_4$ pint/$^2/_3$ cup vegetable stock
115 g/4 oz/$^1/_2$ cup red or green lentils
400 g/14 oz can chopped tomatoes
30 ml/2 tbsp concentrated tomato
    purée
5 ml/1 tsp fresh thyme
5 ml/1 tsp chopped fresh rosemary
40 g/1$^1/_2$ oz/3 tbsp butter
40 g/1$^1/_2$ oz/$^1/_3$ cup plain flour
600 ml/1 pint/2$^1/_2$ cups milk
large pinch of grated nutmeg
16-18 cannelloni tubes
50 g/2 oz/$^1/_2$ cup grated Cheddar
    cheese
25 g/1 oz/$^1/_3$ cup freshly grated
    Parmesan cheese
25 g/1 oz/$^1/_2$ cup fresh white
    breadcrumbs
salt and freshly ground black pepper
fresh flat leaf parsley, to garnish

1 To make the filling, put the onion, garlic, carrots and celery into a large saucepan, add half the stock, cover and cook for 5 minutes or until tender.

2 Add the lentils, chopped tomatoes, tomato purée, thyme, rosemary and seasoning. Bring to the boil, cover, then simmer for 20 minutes. Remove the lid and cook for about 10 minutes more, until thick and soft. Leave to cool.

3 To make the sauce, melt the butter in a pan, stir in the flour and cook for 2 minutes, then gradually add the milk, whisking until the sauce boils and thickens. Season to taste with salt, pepper and nutmeg.

4 Preheat the oven to 180°C/350°F/ Gas 4. Fill the uncooked cannelloni by piping the filling into each tube. (It is easiest to hold them upright with one end flat on a board, while piping into the other end.)

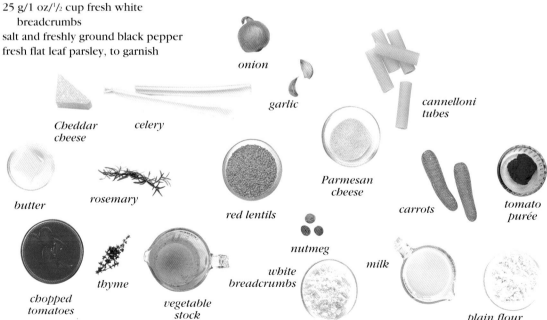

onion

garlic

cannelloni tubes

Cheddar cheese

celery

Parmesan cheese

butter

rosemary

red lentils

carrots

tomato purée

nutmeg

milk

chopped tomatoes

thyme

vegetable stock

white breadcrumbs

plain flour

5 Spoon half the sauce into the bottom of a 20 cm/8 in square ovenproof dish. Lay two rows of filled cannelloni on top and spoon over the remaining sauce.

6 Scatter over the cheeses and breadcrumbs. Bake for 30–40 minutes. Allow to stand for 5 minutes before serving, garnished with flat leaf parsley.

COOK'S TIP
If the topping has not browned when you take the bake out of the oven, finish it under the grill.

Fresh Herb Pizza

This pizza is rich and tasty but couldn't be simpler to make. Cut into thin wedges and serve as part of a mixed antipasti.

Serves 8

INGREDIENTS
115 g/4 oz/2 cups mixed fresh herbs, such as parsley, basil and oregano
3 garlic cloves, crushed
120 ml/4 fl oz/½ cup double cream
1 pizza base, 25–30 cm/10–12 in diameter
15 ml/1 tbsp olive oil
115 g/4 oz freshly grated Pecorino cheese
salt and freshly ground black pepper

double cream

olive oil

Pecorino cheese

basil

garlic

parsley

oregano

pizza base

1 Preheat the oven to 220°C/425°F/ Gas 7. Chop all the herbs, finely. Use a food processor if you have one.

2 Mix the herbs, garlic, cream and seasoning in a bowl.

3 Brush the pizza base with the oil, then spread over the herb mixture.

4 Sprinkle over the Pecorino. Bake for 15–20 minutes until crisp and golden; the topping should still be moist. Cut into thin wedges and serve immediately.

COOK'S TIP
Use garlic oil for brushing the pizza base, if possible. You'll find a recipe on page 17.

Radicchio Pizza

This unusual topping uses chopped radicchio with leeks, tomatoes and Parmesan and mozzarella cheeses. The scone dough base isn't strictly Italian, so substitute a classic pizza base if you prefer.

Serves 2

INGREDIENTS

$^1/_2 \times$ 400 g/14 oz can chopped
    tomatoes
2 garlic cloves, crushed
pinch of dried basil
25 ml/1$^1/_2$ tbsp olive oil,
2 leeks, sliced
100 g/3$^1/_2$ oz radicchio, chopped
20 g/$^3/_4$ oz/$^1/_4$ cup freshly grated
    Parmesan cheese
115 g/4 oz mozzarella cheese, sliced
10-12 stoned black olives
fresh basil leaves, to garnish
salt and freshly ground black pepper

FOR THE DOUGH

225 g/8 oz/2 cups self-raising flour
2.5 ml/$^1/_2$ tsp salt
50 g/2 oz/$^1/_4$ cup butter
about 120 ml/4 fl oz/$^1/_2$ cup milk

chopped tomatoes — garlic — mozzarella cheese — basil — Parmesan cheese — olive oil — leeks — black olives — butter — self-raising flour — milk — radicchio

1 Make the dough. Mix the flour and salt in a bowl, rub in the butter, then gradually stir in the milk and mix to a soft dough.

2 Preheat the oven to 220°C/425°F/ Gas 7. Roll out the dough to a 25–28 cm/10–11 in round. Place on a greased baking sheet. Mix the tomatoes and half the garlic in a saucepan. Add the dried basil and seasoning, and simmer until thick and reduced by about half.

3 Heat most of the olive oil in a large frying pan (retain a little for dipping the basil leaves) and fry the leeks and remaining garlic for 4–5 minutes until slightly softened. Add the radicchio and cook, stirring continuously for a few minutes, then cover and simmer gently for 5–10 minutes. Stir in the Parmesan and season with salt and pepper.

4 Cover the dough base with the tomato mixture and then spoon the leek and radicchio mixture over. Arrange the mozzarella slices on top and scatter over the black olives. Dip a few basil leaves in olive oil, arrange on top and then bake the pizza for 15–20 minutes until the scone base and the top are golden brown.

Spring Vegetable and Pine Nut Pizza

Pine nuts are very popular in Italy, where they are known as *pinoli*. They go very well with fresh young vegetables.

Serves 2-3

INGREDIENTS
1 pizza base, 25-30 cm/10-12 in
   diameter
45ml/3 tbsp olive oil, preferably
   garlic oil (see page 17)
4 spring onions
2 courgettes
1 leek
115 g/4 oz asparagus tips
15 ml/1 tbsp chopped fresh oregano
30 ml/2 tbsp pine nuts
50 g/2 oz mozzarella cheese, grated
30 ml/2 tbsp freshly grated Parmesan
   cheese

FOR THE TOMATO SAUCE
15 ml/1 tbsp olive oil
1 onion, finely chopped
1 garlic clove, crushed
400 g/14 oz can chopped tomatoes
15 ml/1 tbsp tomato purée
15 ml/1 tbsp chopped fresh herbs
pinch of sugar
salt and freshly ground black pepper

onion

fresh herbs

courgettes

leek

tomato purée

garlic

Parmesan

mozzarella

spring onions

pine nuts

chopped tomatoes

asparagus

oregano

pizza base

olive oil

1 Make the tomato sauce. Heat the oil and fry the onion and garlic until soft. Stir in all the remaining ingredients and cook for 20 minutes, stirring often, until thick and flavoursome.

2 Brush the pizza base with 15 ml/1 tbsp of the olive oil, then spread over the tomato sauce. Preheat the oven to 220°C/425°F/Gas 7. Slice the spring onions, courgettes, leek and asparagus.

3 Heat half the remaining olive oil in a frying pan and stir-fry the vegetables for 3–5 minutes.

4 Arrange the vegetables over the tomato sauce. Sprinkle the oregano and pine nuts over the pizza.

5 Mix together the mozzarella and Parmesan cheeses and sprinkle over the pizza. Drizzle with the remaining olive oil and season with black pepper. Bake for 15–20 minutes until crisp and golden. Serve immediately.

Wild Mushroom Pizzettes

Serve these extravagant pizzas as a starter. Fresh wild mushrooms add a distinctive flavour to the topping, but a mixture of cultivated mushrooms such as shiitake, oyster and chestnut mushrooms would do just as well.

Serves 4

INGREDIENTS
45 ml/3 tbsp olive oil
350 g/12 oz/3 cups fresh wild
    mushrooms, sliced
2 shallots, chopped
2 garlic cloves, finely chopped
30 ml/2 tbsp chopped fresh mixed
    thyme and flat leaf parsley
40 g/1½ oz/⅓ cup grated Gruyère
    cheese
30 ml/2 tbsp freshly grated Parmesan
    cheese
salt and freshly ground black pepper

FOR THE DOUGH
150 g/5 oz packet pizza base mix
120 ml/4 fl oz/½ cup lukewarm
    water

parsley

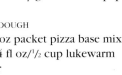
Gruyère
cheese

olive
oil

thyme

Parmesan
cheese

shallots

wild
mushrooms

garlic

1 Preheat the oven to 220°C/425°F/Gas 7. Heat 30 ml/2 tbsp of the oil in a frying pan. Add the mushrooms, shallots and garlic and fry over a medium heat until all the juices have evaporated.

2 Stir in half the herbs and seasoning, then set aside to cool. Make the dough by mixing the contents of the packet with the water, as described on the label. Knead the dough for 5 minutes until smooth and elastic.

3 Divide the dough into 4 pieces and roll out each one on a lightly floured surface to a 13 cm/5 in circle. Place well apart on 2 greased baking sheets, then push up the dough edges to form a thin rim. Brush with the remaining oil, top with the wild mushroom mixture.

4 Sprinkle over the Gruyère and Parmesan cheeses. Bake for 15–20 minutes until crisp and golden. Scatter over the remaining herbs to serve.

New Potato, Rosemary and Garlic Pizza

New potatoes, smoked mozzarella, rosemary and garlic make the flavour of this pizza unique. For a delicious variation, use sage instead of rosemary.

Serves 2-3

INGREDIENTS

350 g/12 oz new potatoes
45 ml/3 tbsp olive oil
2 garlic cloves, crushed
1 pizza base, 25-30 cm/10-12 in
    diameter
1 red onion, thinly sliced
150 g/5 oz smoked mozzarella
    cheese, grated
10 ml/2 tsp chopped fresh rosemary
salt and freshly ground black pepper
30 ml/2 tbsp freshly grated Parmesan
    cheese

olive oil

Parmesan cheese

smoked mozzarella cheese

new potatoes

red onion   rosemary

pizza base

garlic

1 Preheat the oven to 220°C/425°F/ Gas 7. Cook the potatoes in boiling salted water for 5 minutes. Drain well. When cool, peel and slice thinly.

2 Heat 30 ml/2 tbsp of the oil in a frying pan. Add the sliced potatoes and garlic and fry for 5–8 minutes until the potatoes are tender.

3 Brush the pizza base with the remaining oil. Scatter over the onion, then arrange the potatoes on top.

4 Sprinkle over the mozzarella and rosemary. Grind over plenty of black pepper and bake for 15–20 minutes until crisp and golden. Remove from the oven and sprinkle over the Parmesan cheese to serve.

Venetian Leek, Lemon and Mushroom Risotto

A delicious risotto, packed full of flavour, this is a great recipe for an informal supper with friends.

Serves 4

INGREDIENTS

225 g/8 oz trimmed leeks
225 g/8 oz/2–3 cups brown-cap
   mushrooms
30 ml/2 tbsp olive oil
3 garlic cloves, crushed
75 g/3 oz/6 tbsp butter
1 large onion, roughly chopped
350 g/12 oz/scant 1³/₄ cups risotto
   (arborio) rice
1.2 litres/2 pints/5 cups hot vegetable
   stock
grated rind and juice of 1 lemon, plus
   lemon wedges, to serve
50 g/2 oz/²/₃ cup freshly grated
   Parmesan cheese
60 ml/4 tbsp mixed chopped fresh
   chives and flat leaf parsley
salt and freshly ground black pepper

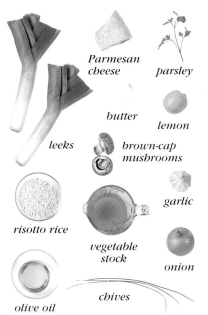

Parmesan cheese   *parsley*
butter   *lemon*
leeks   *brown-cap mushrooms*
risotto rice   *garlic*
vegetable stock   *onion*
olive oil   *chives*

1   Wash the leeks well. Slice in half lengthways and chop roughly. Wipe the mushrooms with kitchen paper and chop them roughly.

2   Heat the oil in a large saucepan and cook the garlic for 1 minute. Add the leeks, mushrooms and plenty of seasoning and cook over a medium heat for about 10 minutes, or until softened and browned. Remove from the pan and set aside.

3   Add 25 g/1 oz of the butter to the pan and cook the onion over a medium heat for about 5 minutes until softened and golden.

4   Stir in the rice and cook for 1 minute until the grains begin to look translucent and are coated in the fat. Add a ladleful of stock to the pan and cook gently, stirring occasionally, until the liquid has been absorbed.

5   Stir in more liquid as each ladleful is absorbed; this should take 20–25 minutes. The risotto will become thick and creamy and the rice should be tender but not sticky.

6   Just before serving, stir in the leeks, mushrooms, remaining butter, grated lemon rind and 45 ml/3 tbsp of the juice. Add half the Parmesan and herbs. Adjust the seasoning and sprinkle with the remaining Parmesan and herbs. Serve with lemon wedges.

Pumpkin and Pistachio Risotto

This combination of creamy golden rice and orange pumpkin tastes as good as it looks. Like all risottos, it originally came from northern Italy.

Serves 4

INGREDIENTS

1.2 litres/2 pints/5 cups vegetable stock or water
generous pinch of saffron threads
30 ml/2 tbsp olive oil
1 onion, chopped
2 garlic cloves, crushed
450 g/1 lb/2⅓ cups risotto (arborio) rice
900 g/2 lb pumpkin, peeled, seeded and cut into 2 cm/¾ in cubes
200 ml/7 fl oz/scant 1 cup dry white wine
45 ml/3 tbsp freshly grated Parmesan cheese
50 g/2 oz/½ cup pistachio nuts
45 ml/3 tbsp chopped fresh marjoram or oregano, plus extra leaves, to garnish
salt, freshly grated nutmeg and freshly ground black pepper

white wine

pumpkin

vegetable stock

olive oil

garlic

saffron

Parmesan cheese

pistachio nuts

risotto rice

onion

marjoram

1 Bring the stock or water to the boil and reduce to a low simmer. Ladle a little stock into a small bowl. Add the saffron threads and leave to infuse.

2 Heat the oil in a large saucepan. Add the onion and garlic and cook gently for about 5 minutes until softened. Add the rice and pumpkin and cook for a few more minutes until the rice looks transparent.

3 Pour in the wine and allow it to bubble hard. When it has been absorbed add a quarter of the stock and the infused saffron and liquid. Stir constantly until all the liquid has been absorbed.

COOK'S TIP
Italian arborio rice must be used to make an authentic risotto. Choose unpolished white arborio as it contains more starch.

4 Add the remaining stock or water, a ladleful at a time, allowing the rice to absorb the liquid before adding more. Stir all the time. After 20–30 minutes the rice should be golden yellow and creamy, and just tender when tested.

5 Stir in the Parmesan cheese, cover the pan and leave to stand for 5 minutes.

6 To finish, stir in the pistachio nuts and marjoram or oregano. Season to taste with a little salt, nutmeg and pepper, and scatter over a few extra marjoram or oregano leaves.

Polenta with Mushroom Sauce

This dish is delicious made with a mixture of wild and cultivated mushrooms.

Serves 6

INGREDIENTS
10 g/¼ oz/2 tbsp dried porcini
  mushrooms (omit if using wild
  mushrooms)
60 ml/4 tbsp olive oil
1 onion, finely chopped
675 g/1½ lb/6 cups mushrooms, wild
  or cultivated, or a combination of
  both, sliced
2 garlic cloves, finely chopped
45ml/3 tbsp chopped fresh flat leaf
  parsley
3 tomatoes, peeled and diced
15 ml/1 tbsp concentrated tomato
  purée
175 ml/6 fl oz/¾ cup warm vegetable
  stock
1.5 ml/¼ tsp fresh thyme leaves,
  or 1 large pinch dried thyme
1 bay leaf
350 g/12 oz/2½ cups polenta
1.5 litres/2½ pints/6¼ cups water
salt and freshly ground black pepper
fresh parsley sprigs, to garnish

bay leaf   *onion*   *garlic*

mushrooms   *vegetable stock*   *tomatoes*   *olive oil*

thyme   *parsley*   *polenta*

porcini mushrooms   *tomato purée*

1 Soak the dried mushrooms, if using, in a small bowl of warm water for about 20 minutes. Remove the mushrooms and rinse them well in several changes of cold water. Filter the soaking water through a layer of kitchen paper placed in a sieve and reserve.

2 In a large frying pan, heat the oil and sauté the onion over a low heat until soft and golden.

4 Soften the tomato purée in the warm stock (use only 120 ml/4 fl oz/ ½ cup stock if using dried mushrooms). Add the purée to the pan with the herbs. Add the dried mushrooms and soaking liquid, if using, and season. Reduce the heat to low and cook for 15–20 minutes. Set aside.

3 Add the fresh mushrooms to the pan. Stir over a medium to high heat until they give up their liquid. Add the garlic, parsley and diced tomatoes. Cook for 4–5 minutes.

5 Bring the measured water to the boil in a large, heavy saucepan. Add 15 ml/1 tbsp salt. Reduce the heat to a simmer and slowly add the polenta in a fine, steady stream. Stir constantly with a whisk until all the polenta has been incorporated.

6 Switch to a long-handled wooden spoon and continue to stir the polenta over a low to medium heat until it is a thick mass and pulls away from the sides of the pan. This may take 25–50 minutes, depending on the type of polenta used. For best results, never stop stirring the polenta until you remove it from the heat. When the polenta has almost finished cooking, gently reheat the mushroom sauce.

7 To serve, spoon the polenta on to a warmed serving platter. Make a well in the centre. Spoon some of the mushroom sauce into the well, and garnish with fresh parsley sprigs. Serve at once, handing round the remaining sauce in a separate bowl.

Spinach and Ricotta Gnocchi

Gnocchi are irresistible little dumplings made from semolina or a mixture of mashed potato and flour. This version mixes both semolina and potato with ricotta and Parmesan cheeses.

Serves 4

INGREDIENTS

175 g/6 oz/2 cups cold mashed
    potato
75 g/3 oz/¹/₂ cup semolina
115 g/4 oz/1 cup frozen leaf spinach,
    thawed, squeezed and chopped
115 g/4 oz/¹/₂ cup ricotta cheese
50 g/2 oz/²/₃ cup freshly grated
    Parmesan cheese
30 ml/2 tbsp beaten egg
2.5 ml/¹/₂ tsp salt
large pinch of grated nutmeg
freshly ground black pepper
fresh basil sprigs, to garnish

FOR THE BUTTER

75 g/3 oz/6 tbsp butter
5 ml/1 tsp grated lemon rind
15 ml/1 tbsp lemon juice
15 ml/1 tbsp chopped fresh basil

mashed potato *semolina* *spinach*

ricotta cheese *Parmesan cheese* *lemon*

basil *egg* *butter*

1 Place all the gnocchi ingredients except the basil in a bowl and mix well. Take pieces of the mixture the size of a walnut, and roll back and forth a few times along the prongs of a fork until ridged. Repeat to make 28 gnocchi. Lay them on a tray lined with clear film.

2 Drop the gnocchi into a large pan of simmering water.

3 Simmer the gnocchi for about 1 minute after they have risen to the surface of the water, then remove them with a slotted spoon and transfer to a lightly greased ovenproof dish. Sprinkle the gnocchi with a little Parmesan cheese and grill for 2 minutes, or until lightly browned.

4 Meanwhile, heat the butter in a pan and stir in the lemon rind and juice, basil and seasoning. Pour a quarter of the hot butter over each portion of gnocchi and garnish with fresh basil. Serve hot.

Potato and Red Pepper Frittata

Fresh herbs make all the difference in this simple but delicious recipe – parsley or chives could be substituted for the chopped mint.

Serves 3-4

INGREDIENTS
450 g/1 lb small new potatoes
6 eggs
30 ml/2 tbsp chopped fresh mint,
    plus fresh mint sprigs, to garnish
30 ml/2 tbsp olive oil
1 onion, chopped
2 garlic cloves, crushed
2 red peppers, seeded and roughly
    chopped
salt and freshly ground black pepper

eggs

new
potatoes

olive
oil

onion

garlic

red
peppers

mint

1 Cook the potatoes in a pan of boiling salted water until just tender. Drain, leave to cool slightly, then cut into thick slices.

2 Whisk together the eggs, mint and seasoning in a bowl, then set aside. Next, heat the oil in a large frying pan. Add the onion, garlic, peppers and potatoes to the pan and cook, stirring gently, for 5 minutes.

3 Pour the egg mixture over the vegetables and stir gently. Cook over a medium heat. As the mixture cooks, push it to the centre of the pan to allow the liquid egg to run on to the base.

4 Continue to move the mixture until the eggs start to set. Cook for 1–2 minutes more, without stirring, then place the pan under a hot grill to brown the top of the frittata lightly. Serve hot, warm or cold, cut into wedges and garnished with sprigs of mint.

Potatoes Baked with Tomatoes

This simple, hearty dish from the south of Italy is best when fresh tomatoes are at their prime. Buy fat, juicy beefsteak tomatoes, if you can get them.

Serves 6

INGREDIENTS

90 ml/6 tbsp olive oil
2 large red or yellow onions, thinly
    sliced
900 g/2 lb potatoes, thinly sliced
450 g/1 lb tomatoes, sliced
115 g/4 oz/1 cup freshly grated
    Parmesan or mature Cheddar
    cheese
a few leaves of fresh basil
60 ml/4 tbsp water
salt and freshly ground black pepper

olive oil

red onions

potatoes

tomatoes

Parmesan cheese

basil

1 Preheat the oven to 180°C/350°F/Gas 4. Brush a large baking dish generously with oil. Arrange a layer of onions in the dish, followed by layers of potatoes and tomatoes.

2 Pour on a little of the oil, and sprinkle with the cheese. Season well. Repeat until all the vegetables have been used, ending with an overlapping layer of potatoes and tomatoes. Tear the basil leaves into pieces, and tuck them among the vegetables.

3 Sprinkle the top with cheese, and drizzle with a little oil. Pour on the water, taking care not to disturb the cheese topping too much. Bake for 1 hour, or until tender.

4 If the top begins to brown too much, place a sheet of greaseproof paper, foil or a baking sheet on top of the dish. Serve hot.

Gorgonzola, Cauliflower and Walnut Gratin

When Italians make cauliflower cheese, they transform a humble dish into something sublime.

Serves 4

INGREDIENTS

1 large cauliflower, broken into
   florets
25 g/1 oz/2 tbsp butter
1 medium onion, finely chopped
45 ml/3 tbsp plain flour
450 ml/³/₄ pint/1³/₄ cups milk
150 g/5 oz Gorgonzola or other blue
   cheese, cut into pieces
2.5 ml/¹/₂ tsp celery salt
pinch of cayenne pepper
75 g/3 oz/³/₄ cup chopped walnuts
pinch of salt
fresh flat leaf parsley, to garnish

butter

Gorgonzola cheese

cauliflower

walnuts

flour

milk

onion

1 Bring a large saucepan of salted water to the boil and cook the cauliflower for 6 minutes. Drain and place in a flameproof gratin dish.

2 Heat the butter in a heavy saucepan. Add the onion and cook over a low heat to soften without colouring. Stir in the flour. Cook for 1–2 minutes, then gradually add the milk, stirring constantly until the sauce boils and thickens. Stir in the cheese, celery salt and cayenne pepper.

3 Spoon the sauce over the cauliflower, scatter with the chopped walnuts and cook under a moderately hot grill until golden. Garnish with the parsley and serve.

VARIATIONS

For a delicious alternative, replace cauliflower with 1.2 kg/2¹/₂ lb fresh broccoli or combine the two. Cooked pasta can be mixed with the vegetables and sauce, if you like. This works best with small shapes like elbow macaroni or penne.

Courgettes with Sun-dried Tomatoes

One way to preserve tomatoes for winter is to dry them in the sun, as they do all over southern Italy. These tomatoes have a concentrated, sweet flavour that goes well with courgettes.

Serves 6

INGREDIENTS
10 sun-dried tomatoes
175 ml/6 fl oz/³/₄ cup warm water
75 ml/5 tbsp olive oil
1 large onion, finely sliced
2 cloves garlic, finely chopped
900 g/2 lb courgettes, cut into thin
    strips
salt and freshly ground black pepper

sun-dried
tomatoes

olive
oil

garlic

onion

courgettes

1 Slice the tomatoes into thin strips. Place in a bowl with the warm water. Leave to soak for 20 minutes.

2 Heat the oil in a large frying pan and add the onion. Cook over low to medium heat, stirring, until the onion softens; do not let it brown.

3 Stir in the garlic and the courgettes. Cook for about 5 minutes, continuing to stir the mixture.

4 Stir in the tomatoes and their soaking liquid. Season with salt and pepper. Raise the heat slightly and cook until the courgettes are just tender. Serve hot or cold.

COOK'S TIP

Use sun-dried tomatoes in oil, if you prefer, in which case it will not be necessary to soak them in water. Use a little of the oil from the jar for frying the onion and add 120 ml/ 4 fl oz/¹/₂ cup water or tomato juice when adding the tomatoes to the courgette mixture.

Asparagus with Eggs

The addition of fried eggs and grated Parmesan turns simple boiled asparagus into something special. Peeling ensures the asparagus cooks evenly, and makes the whole spear edible.

Serves 4

INGREDIENTS
450 g/1 lb fresh asparagus
65 g/2½ oz/5 tbsp butter
4 eggs
60 ml/4 tbsp freshly grated Parmesan
   cheese
salt and freshly ground black pepper

butter

eggs

Parmesan cheese

asparagus

1 Cut off any woody ends from the asparagus. Peel the lower half of the spears by inserting a knife under the thick skin at the base, and pulling upwards towards the tip.

2 Cook the asparagus in boiling salted water until just tender when pierced with a knife. Meanwhile, melt about a third of the butter in a frying pan. When it is bubbling, gently break in the eggs one at a time, and cook them until the whites have set, but the yolks are soft.

3 As soon as the asparagus is cooked, remove it from the water with two slotted spoons. Place it on a cake rack covered with a clean dish towel to drain. Divide the spears among warmed individual serving plates. Place a fried egg on each, and sprinkle with the grated Parmesan cheese.

4 Melt the remaining butter in the frying pan. As soon as it is bubbling pour it over the cheese and eggs on the asparagus. Serve at once, handing out salt and pepper separately so that guests can help themselves.

Baked Fennel with Parmesan Cheese

Fennel is widely eaten in Italy, both raw and cooked. Baking softens the aniseed flavour.

Serves 4-6

INGREDIENTS
900 g/2 lb fennel bulbs, cut in half
50 g/2 oz/¼ cup butter
40 g/1½ oz/½ cup freshly grated
   Parmesan cheese

fennel

butter

Parmesan cheese

1 Preheat the oven to 200°C/400°F/ Gas 6. Cook the fennel in a large pan of boiling water until tender but not mushy. Drain.

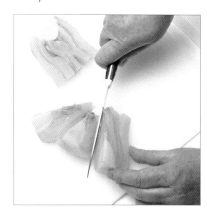

2 Cut the fennel bulbs lengthwise into four or six pieces. Place them in a buttered baking dish. Dot with butter. Sprinkle with the grated Parmesan cheese. Bake for about 20 minutes, until the cheese is golden brown. Serve at once.

VARIATION
For a crunchy texture, sprinkle flaked almonds over the fennel before topping with the Parmesan cheese.

Roast Mushroom Caps with Parsley

Large cap mushrooms have a succulent flavour and a firm texture.

Serves 4

INGREDIENTS
4 large mushrooms, stems removed.
2 garlic cloves, chopped
45 ml/3 tbsp finely chopped fresh
   parsley
olive oil, for sprinkling
salt and freshly ground black pepper

large mushrooms

garlic

parsley

olive oil

1 Preheat the oven to 190°C/375°F/ Gas 5. Oil a baking dish large enough to hold the mushrooms in one layer. Place the mushroom caps in the dish, smooth side down. Mix the garlic with the parsley and spoon into the caps.

2 Season the mushrooms with salt and pepper. Sprinkle the parsley stuffing with oil. Bake for 20–25 minutes. Serve at once.

COOK'S TIP
Although expensive, wild mushrooms have a stronger flavour than the cheaper cultivated variety.

Marinated Vegetable Antipasti

This combination of marinated vegetables makes a particularly delicious starter.

Serves 4

INGREDIENTS

FOR THE PEPPERS
3 red peppers
3 yellow peppers
4 garlic cloves, sliced
handful of fresh basil
extra virgin olive oil
salt and freshly ground black pepper

FOR THE MUSHROOMS
450 g/1 lb/4 cups open cap
    mushrooms, thickly sliced
60 ml/4 tbsp extra virgin olive oil
1 large garlic clove, crushed
15 ml/1 tbsp chopped fresh
    rosemary, plus sprigs, to garnish
250 ml/8 fl oz/1 cup dry white wine

FOR THE OLIVES
1 dried red chilli, crushed
grated rind of 1 lemon, and lemon
    wedge to serve
120 ml/4 fl oz/¹/₂ cup virgin olive oil
225 g/8 oz/1¹/₃ cups black olives
30 ml/2 tbsp chopped flat leaf parsley

yellow peppers
red peppers
garlic
basil
mushrooms
olive oil
rosemary
chilli
parsley
dry white wine
black olives
lemon

1 Grill the peppers until they are blackened and blistered all over. Remove from the heat and place in a large plastic bag. Seal and leave to cool.

2 When cool, peel, then halve, the peppers and remove the seeds. Cut the flesh into strips lengthways and place in a bowl with the garlic and basil. Add salt to taste, cover with oil and marinate for 3–4 hours, tossing occasionally. When serving, garnish with more basil leaves.

3 Place the mushrooms in a bowl. Heat the oil in a small pan and add the garlic, rosemary and wine. Bring to the boil, then simmer for 3 minutes. Season to taste. Pour the mixture over the mushrooms, mix well. When cool, cover and marinate overnight. Serve at room temperature, garnished with rosemary.

4 Prepare the olives. Place the chilli and lemon rind in a small pan with the oil. Heat gently for about 3 minutes. Add the olives and heat for 1 minute more. Tip into a bowl and leave to cool. Marinate overnight. Sprinkle with parsley and serve with the lemon wedge.

Garden Salad and Garlic Crostini

Dress a colourful mixture of salad leaves with good olive oil and freshly squeezed lemon juice, then top it with crispy crostini.

Serves 4-6

INGREDIENTS

120 ml/4 fl oz/$\frac{1}{2}$ cup extra virgin
    olive oil
3 thick slices day-old ciabatta, cut
    into 1 cm/$\frac{1}{2}$ in dice
1 garlic clove, halved
$\frac{1}{2}$ small cos lettuce
$\frac{1}{2}$ small oakleaf lettuce
25 g/1 oz rocket leaves or cress
25 g/1 oz/$\frac{1}{3}$ cup fresh flat leaf parsley
juice of 1 fresh lemon
a few flowers of pansies, nasturtiums
    or pot marigolds
a small handful of young dandelion
    leaves
sea salt flakes and freshly ground
    black pepper

olive oil

garlic

parsley

lemon juice

rocket

oakleaf lettuce

cos lettuce

edible flowers

ciabatta

dandelion leaves

1 Heat half the oil and fry the bread cubes until they are lightly browned. Remove the crostini with a slotted spoon, drain on kitchen paper and cool.

2 Rub the inside of a large salad bowl with the garlic and discard. Pour the rest of the oil into the bottom of the bowl.

3 Tear the leaves into bite size pieces and pile them into the bowl. Add the parsley and season the mixture with salt and pepper. Cover and keep chilled until ready to serve.

4 To serve, toss the leaves in the oil in the bowl, then sprinkle with the lemon juice and toss again. Add the flowers and toss very gently. Scatter over the crostini and serve immediately.

Fennel, Orange and Rocket Salad

This light and refreshing salad is ideal to serve with spicy or rich foods.

Serves 4

INGREDIENTS
2 oranges
1 fennel bulb, very thinly sliced
115 g/4 oz rocket leaves
50 g/2 oz/⅓ cup black olives

FOR THE DRESSING
30 ml/2 tbsp extra virgin olive oil
10–15 ml/2–3 tsp balsamic vinegar
1 small garlic clove, crushed
salt and freshly ground black pepper

oranges
fennel
rocket
black olives
garlic
balsamic vinegar
olive oil

1 With a vegetable peeler, cut strips of rind from the oranges and cut into thin strips. Cook in boiling water for a few minutes. Drain. Peel and slice the oranges, removing all the white pith. Mix the oranges and fennel in a serving bowl and toss with the rocket leaves.

2 Whisk the oil, vinegar, garlic and seasoning together; pour over the salad, toss well and leave to stand for a few minutes. Sprinkle with the black olives and strips of pared orange rind.

COOK'S TIP
Slice the fennel lengthways, preferably in a food processor fitted with a slicing disc.

Aubergine, Lemon and Caper Salad

This classic Sicilian dish is delicious with pasta or simply on its own with some good crusty bread.

Serves 4

INGREDIENTS
1 large aubergine, about 675 g/1½ lb
60 ml/4 tbsp olive oil
grated rind and juice of 1 lemon
30 ml/2 tbsp drained bottled capers, rinsed
12 stoned green olives
30 ml/2 tbsp chopped fresh flat leaf parsley
salt and freshly ground black pepper

aubergine
olive oil
lemon
capers
parsley
green olives

1 Cut the aubergine into 2.5 cm/1 in cubes. Heat the olive oil in a large frying pan and cook the aubergine cubes over a medium heat for about 10 minutes, tossing regularly, until golden and softened. You may need to do this in two batches. Drain on kitchen paper and sprinkle with a little salt.

2 Place the aubergine cubes in a large serving bowl, toss with the lemon rind and juice, capers, olives and chopped parsley and season well with pepper. Taste and add salt only if needed. Serve at room temperature.

COOK'S TIP
This will taste even better when made the day before. Serve at room temperature. If covered, it can be kept in the fridge for up to 4 days.

Summer Pasta Salad

Tender young vegetables in a light dressing make a delicious lunch.

Serves 2-3

INGREDIENTS

225 g/8 oz/2 cups fusilli or other
  dried pasta shapes
3 baby carrots, halved
6 baby sweetcorn cobs, halved
  lengthways
50 g/2 oz/½ cup mange touts
115 g/4 oz young asparagus spears,
  trimmed
4 spring onions, shredded
10 ml/2 tsp white wine vinegar
60 ml/4 tbsp extra virgin olive oil
15 ml/1 tbsp wholegrain mustard
salt and freshly ground black pepper

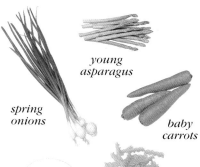

*young
asparagus*

*spring
onions*

*baby
carrots*

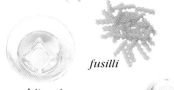

fusilli

*white wine
vinegar*

*olive
oil*

*baby
sweetcorn*

*wholegrain
mustard*

mange touts

1 Cook the pasta in boiling salted water, following the instructions on the packet. Meanwhile, cook the carrots and sweetcorn in a second pan of boiling salted water for 5 minutes.

2 Add the mange touts and asparagus to the carrot mixture and cook for 2–3 minutes more. Drain all the vegetables and refresh under cold running water. Drain again.

3 Tip the vegetable mixture into a mixing bowl, add the spring onions and toss well together.

4 Drain the pasta, refresh it under cold running water and drain again. Toss with the vegetables. Mix the vinegar, olive oil and mustard in a jar. Add salt and pepper to taste, close the jar tightly and shake well. Pour the dressing over the salad. Toss well and serve.

Wholemeal Pasta, Asparagus and Potato Salad with Parmesan Cheese

A meal in itself, this is a real treat when made with fresh asparagus just in season.

Serves 4

INGREDIENTS

350 g/12 oz baby new potatoes
225 g/8 oz/2 cups wholemeal pasta
  shapes
60 ml/4 tbsp extra virgin olive oil
225 g/8 oz fresh asparagus
115 g/4 oz piece fresh Parmesan
  cheese
salt and freshly ground black pepper

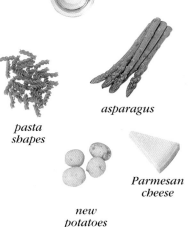

olive oil

asparagus

pasta shapes

Parmesan cheese

new potatoes

1 Cook the potatoes in boiling salted water for 12–15 minutes or until tender. Drain well.

2 Cook the pasta in boiling salted water following the instructions on the packet. Drain well, tip into a bowl with the olive oil, salt and pepper. Add in the potatoes and toss while still warm.

3 Trim any woody ends off the asparagus and halve the stalks if very long. Cook in boiling salted water for 6 minutes until bright green and still crunchy. Drain. Plunge into cold water to prevent further cooking and allow to cool. Drain and dry on kitchen paper.

4 Toss the asparagus with the potatoes and pasta, season and transfer to a shallow bowl. Using a vegetable peeler, shave the Parmesan cheese over the salad.

COOK'S TIP

Look out for speciality salad potatoes like Linzer Delikatess, Belle de Fontanay and Charlotte.

Marsala Carrots

The sweet flavour of marsala goes surprisingly well with carrots in this Sicilian dish.

Serves 4

INGREDIENTS
50 g/2 oz/¼ cup butter
450 g/1 lb carrots, thinly sliced
5 ml/1 tsp granulated sugar
2.5 ml/½ tsp salt
60 ml/4 tbsp marsala

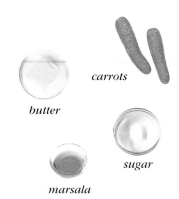

carrots

butter

sugar

marsala

1 Melt the butter in a medium saucepan, and add the carrots. Stir well to coat. Add the sugar and salt, mix well, then stir in the marsala, and simmer for 4–5 minutes.

2 Pour in enough water to barely cover the carrots. Cover the pan, and cook over a low to medium heat until the carrots are tender. Remove the lid and cook until almost all the liquid has disappeared. Serve hot.

Broccoli with Garlic

This is a simple way of transforming lightly cooked broccoli into a succulent Mediterranean dish.

Serves 6

INGREDIENTS
900 g/2 lb fresh broccoli
90 ml/6 tbsp olive oil
2–3 garlic cloves, finely chopped
salt and freshly ground black pepper

broccoli

garlic

olive oil

1 Cut off any woody parts at the base of the broccoli stems, then peel the remaining stems. Cut any very long or wide stalks in half. Cook in boiling salted water for 5–6 minutes until just tender. Drain well.

2 In a frying pan large enough to hold all the broccoli pieces, gently heat the oil with the garlic. When the garlic is light golden (do not let it brown or it will be bitter) add the broccoli, and cook over medium heat for 3–4 minutes, turning carefully to coat it with the hot oil. Season with salt and pepper. Serve hot or cold.

Stuffed Peppers

Italian cooks make marvellous use of sweet, juicy peppers. This wonderful recipe for stuffed peppers comes from the north.

Serves 6

INGREDIENTS

6 medium to large peppers, any colour
200 g/7 oz/1 cup long grain rice
60 ml/4 tbsp olive oil
1 large onion, finely chopped
2 garlic cloves, finely chopped
3 tomatoes, peeled and cut into small dice
60 ml/4 tbsp white wine
45 ml/3 tbsp finely chopped fresh flat leaf parsley
115 g/4 oz mozzarella cheese, cut into small dice
90 ml/6 tbsp freshly grated Parmesan cheese
salt and freshly ground black pepper

peppers

rice

garlic

olive oil

white wine

tomatoes

mozzarella cheese

parsley

onion

Parmesan cheese

1 Cut the tops off the peppers. Scoop out the seeds and fibrous insides. Blanch the peppers and their tops in a large pan of boiling water for 3–4 minutes. Remove, and stand upside down on racks to drain.

2 Cook the rice in boiling salted water following the instructions on the packet, but drain and rinse it in cold water 3 minutes before the recommended cooking time has elapsed. Drain again.

3 Heat the oil in a frying pan and sauté the onion until soft. Stir in the garlic, tomatoes and wine; cook for 5 minutes.

4 Preheat the oven to 190°C/375°F/ Gas 5. Remove the tomato mixture from the heat. Stir in the rice, parsley, mozzarella cheese and 60 ml/4 tbsp of the Parmesan cheese. Season the mixture with salt and pepper.

5 Pat the insides of the peppers dry with paper towels. Sprinkle with salt and pepper. Stuff the peppers. Sprinkle the tops with the remaining Parmesan, and drizzle with a little oil.

6 Arrange the peppers in a shallow baking dish. Pour in enough water to come 1 cm/½ inch up the sides of the peppers. Bake for 25 minutes. Serve at once, with home-made tomato sauce if you like. These peppers are also good served at room temperature.

Lemon Ricotta Cake

This cake from Sardinia is very different from a traditional cheesecake, but it is even more tasty.

Serves 6-8

INGREDIENTS
75 g/3 oz/6 tbsp butter, softened
175 g/6 oz/³/₄ cup granulated sugar
75 g/3 oz/scant ¹/₂ cup ricotta cheese
3 eggs, separated
175 g/6 oz/1¹/₂ cups self-raising flour
grated rind of 1 lemon
45 ml/3 tbsp fresh lemon juice
icing sugar, for dusting

butter   ricotta cheese   eggs

self-raising flour   lemon   icing sugar

sugar

1 Preheat the oven to 180°C/350°F/ Gas 4. Grease and line a 23 cm/9 in round springform cake tin. Cream the butter with the sugar, then beat in the ricotta, egg yolks, flour, lemon rind and juice until evenly mixed.

2 Beat the egg whites stiffly. Fold them carefully into the mixture. Spoon it into the prepared tin. Bake for 45 minutes, or until a skewer inserted in the cake comes out clean. Allow the cake to cool in the tin for 10 minutes before turning it out on to a rack to cool completely. Dust generously with icing sugar before serving.

Peaches with Amaretti

Peaches are plentiful all over Italy. They are sometimes prepared hot, as in this classic dish.

Serves 4

INGREDIENTS
65 g/2¹/₂ oz/²/₃ cup crushed amaretti
   biscuits
30 ml/2 tbsp marsala
25 g/1 oz/2 tbsp butter, softened
2.5 ml/¹/₂ tsp vanilla essence
30 ml/2 tbsp granulated sugar
1 egg yolk
4 ripe fresh peaches, halved and
   stoned
juice of ¹/₂ lemon

butter   egg   lemon juice

marsala

amaretti biscuits

vanilla essence

sugar   peaches

1 Preheat the oven to 180°C/350°F/ Gas 4. Soften the amaretti crumbs in the marsala for a few minutes. Beat the butter until soft. Stir in the soaked amaretti crumbs, then add the vanilla essence, sugar and egg yolk.

2 Enlarge the hollow left by the stone in each peach half by scraping out some of the flesh. Sprinkle the peach halves with the lemon juice and arrange them in a baking dish. Divide the amaretti mixture among them. Bake for 35–40 minutes. Stuffed peaches are delicious hot or cold.

Pine Nut Tart

This traditional Italian tart has a delectable nut filling over a layer of raspberry jam in a rich pastry case.

Serves 8

INGREDIENTS
115 g/4 oz/$\frac{1}{2}$ cup butter, softened
115 g/4 oz/$\frac{1}{2}$ cup caster sugar
1 egg, plus 2 egg yolks
150 g/5 oz/$1\frac{2}{3}$ cups ground almonds
115 g/4 oz/$1\frac{1}{3}$ cups pine nuts
60 ml/4 tbsp seedless raspberry jam
icing sugar, for dusting
whipped cream, to serve

FOR THE PASTRY
175 g/6 oz/$1\frac{1}{2}$ cups plain flour
75 ml/5 tbsp caster sugar
1.5 ml/$\frac{1}{4}$ tsp baking powder
pinch of salt
115 g/4 oz/$\frac{1}{2}$ cup chilled butter, diced
1 egg yolk

butter

caster sugar

eggs

pine nuts

icing sugar

flour

baking powder

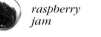
ground almonds

raspberry jam

COOK'S TIP

This pastry is too sticky to roll out, so simply mould it into the bottom and sides of the tin with your fingertips.

1 Make the pastry. Sift the flour, sugar, baking powder and salt on to a cold work surface. Make a well in the centre and put in the diced butter and egg yolk. Gradually work the flour into the butter and egg yolk, using your fingertips.

2 Gather the dough together, then press it evenly into a 23 cm/9 in fluted tart tin with a removable base. Chill for 30 minutes.

3 Preheat the oven to 160°C/325°F/ Gas 3. Make the filling. Cream the butter with the sugar until light and fluffy, then beat in the egg and egg yolks a little at a time, alternating them with the ground almonds. Beat in the pine nuts.

4 Spread the jam over the pastry base, then spoon in the filling. Bake for 30–35 minutes or until a skewer inserted in the centre of the tart comes out clean. Cool on a wire rack then remove the side of the tin, dust the tart with icing sugar and serve with whipped cream.

Tiramisu

The name of this popular dessert translates as "pick me up", which is said to derive from the fact that it is so good that it literally makes you swoon when you eat it.

Serves 6-8

INGREDIENTS

3 eggs, separated
450 g/1 lb/2 cups mascarpone
   cheese, at room temperature
1 sachet of vanilla sugar
175 ml/6 fl oz/³⁄₄ cup cold, very
   strong, black coffee
120 ml/4 fl oz/¹⁄₂ cup Kahlúa or other
   coffee-flavoured liqueur
18 savoiardi (Italian sponge fingers)
sifted cocoa powder and grated
   bittersweet chocolate, to finish

mascarpone cheese

eggs

Kahlúa

black coffee

cocoa

chocolate

sponge fingers

vanilla sugar

1 Put the egg whites in a grease-free bowl and whisk with an electric mixer. You can tell that the mixture is ready once stiff peaks form.

2 Whisk the mascarpone cheese, vanilla sugar and egg yolks in a separate large bowl until evenly combined. Fold in the egg whites, then put a few spoonfuls of the mixture in the bottom of a large serving bowl and spread it out evenly.

3 Mix the coffee and liqueur in a shallow dish. Dip a sponge finger in the mixture, turn it quickly so that it becomes saturated but does not disintegrate, and place it on top of the mascarpone in the bowl. Add five more dipped sponge fingers, placing them side by side.

4 Spoon in about one-third of the remaining mixture and spread it out. Make more layers in the same way, ending with mascarpone. Level the surface, then sift cocoa powder all over. Cover and chill overnight. Before serving, sprinkle with more cocoa, and grated chocolate.

Zabaglione

This sumptuous warm dessert is easy to make, but it does need to be served straight away. For a dinner party, assemble all the ingredients and equipment ahead of time so that all you have to do is mix everything together after the main course.

Serves 6

INGREDIENTS
4 egg yolks
75 ml/5 tbsp caster sugar
120 ml/4 fl oz/½ cup dry marsala
savoiardi (Italian sponge fingers),
    to serve

eggs

caster sugar

marsala

1 Half fill a pan with water and bring it to simmering point. Put the egg yolks and sugar in a large heatproof bowl and beat with a hand-held electric mixer until pale and creamy.

2 Put the bowl over the pan and gradually pour in the marsala, whisking the mixture until it is very thick and has increased in volume. Immediately pour the zabaglione into six heatproof, long-stemmed glasses. Serve at once, with sponge fingers.

COOK'S TIP

When whisking the egg yolks, make sure that the bottom of the bowl does not touch the water or the egg yolks will scramble.

Lovers' Knots

The literal translation of cenci is "rags and tatters", but they are often referred to by the more endearing term of lovers' knots. They are eaten at carnival time in February.

Makes 24

INGREDIENTS
150 g/5 oz/1¼ cups plain flour
2.5 ml/½ tsp baking powder
pinch of salt
30 ml/2 tbsp caster sugar, plus extra
    for dusting
1 egg, beaten
about 25 ml/1½ tbsp rum
vegetable oil, for deep frying

baking
powder

flour

egg   caster
           sugar

oil   rum

1 Sift the flour, baking powder and salt into a bowl, then stir in the sugar. Add the egg. Mix, then add the rum gradually and continue mixing until the dough draws together. Knead the dough lightly until smooth, then quarter.

2 Roll each piece out to a 15 × 7.5 cm/6 × 3 in rectangle, then cut length-ways into six strips, 1 cm/½ in wide, and tie into a knot. Heat the oil in a deep-fat fryer to 190°C/375°F. Deep fry the knots in batches for 1–2 minutes until crisp and golden. Drain on kitchen paper and serve warm, dusted with sugar.

COOK'S TIP

If you do not have a suitable thermometer, test the temperature of the oil by dropping in a scrap of the dough – it should turn crisp and golden in about 30 seconds.

Sun-dried Tomato Bread

In the south of Italy, tomatoes are often dried in the hot summer sun. They are then preserved in oil, or hung up in strings in the kitchen, to use in the winter.

Makes 4 small loaves

INGREDIENTS
675 g/1½ lb/6 cups strong white
   flour
10 ml/2 tsp salt
25 g/1 oz/2 tbsp caster sugar
25 g/1 oz fresh yeast
400–475 ml/14–16 fl oz/1⅔–2 cups
   warm milk
15 ml/1 tbsp concentrated tomato
   purée
75 g/3 oz/¾ cup drained sun-dried
   tomatoes, chopped, plus 75 ml/
   5 tbsp oil from the jar
75 ml/5 tbsp olive oil
1 large onion, chopped

caster sugar

strong white flour

onion

fresh yeast

milk

tomato purée

olive oil

sun-dried tomatoes

salt

1 Sift the flour, salt and sugar into a bowl, and make a well in the centre. Crumble the yeast into a jug, mix with 150 ml/¼ pint/⅔ cup of the warm milk and add to the flour.

2 Stir the tomato purée into the remaining milk, until evenly blended, then add to the flour with the oil from the sun-dried tomatoes and the olive oil.

3 Gradually mix the flour into the liquid ingredients to form a dough. Knead on a lightly floured surface for 10 minutes, until smooth and elastic. Return to the clean bowl, cover with a cloth, and leave to rise in a warm place for about 2 hours.

4 Knock the dough back and add the sun-dried tomatoes and onion. Knead until evenly distributed. Shape the dough into four rounds and place on a greased baking sheet. Cover with clear film and leave to rise again for about 45 minutes. Preheat the oven to 190°C/375°F/Gas 5. Bake for 45 minutes, or until the loaves sound hollow when you tap them underneath. Cool on a wire rack.

COOK'S TIP
Eat this bread warm, or toasted with grated mozzarella cheese on top.

Walnut Bread

The nutty flavour of this wonderfully textured bread is excellent. Try it toasted and topped with melting goat's cheese for a mouth-watering snack.

Makes 2 loaves

INGREDIENTS

600 g/1 lb 6 oz/5½ cups strong white flour
10 ml/2 tsp salt
10 ml/2 tsp easy-blend dried yeast
150 g/5 oz/1¼ cups chopped walnuts
60 ml/4 tbsp chopped fresh flat leaf parsley
400 ml/14 fl oz/1⅔ cups lukewarm water
60 ml/4 tbsp olive oil

strong white flour

olive oil

walnuts

easy-blend yeast

salt

parsley

1 Sift the flour and salt into a large mixing bowl. Stir in the yeast, walnuts and parsley.

2 Make a well in the centre of the dry ingredients. Pour in the water and oil and mix to a soft dough. Knead on a lightly floured surface for about 10 minutes until smooth and elastic. Place in a greased bowl, cover and leave in a warm place for about 1 hour until doubled in bulk.

3 Knock back and knead the dough for 2–3 minutes. Divide in half and shape each piece into a thick roll about 18–20 cm/7–8 in long. Place on greased baking sheets, cover with clear film and leave to rise for about 30 minutes.

4 Meanwhile, preheat the oven to 220°C/425°F/Gas 7. Remove the clear film, then lightly slash the top of each loaf. Bake for 10 minutes, then reduce the oven temperature to 180°C/350°F/Gas 4 and bake for 25–30 minutes more, until the loaves sound hollow when tapped underneath. Serve warm.

Rosemary and Sea Salt Focaccia

An Italian flat bread made with olive oil, focaccia is now famous the world over. Here it is given added flavour with rosemary and coarse sea salt.

Makes 1 loaf

INGREDIENTS
350 g/12 oz/3 cups strong white flour
2.5 ml/½ tsp salt
10 ml/2 tsp easy-blend dried yeast
about 250 ml/8 fl oz/1 cup lukewarm
    water
45ml/3 tbsp olive oil
1 small red onion
leaves from 1 large fresh rosemary
    sprig
5 ml/1 tsp coarse sea salt

coarse sea salt

water

olive oil

easy-blend yeast

strong white flour

red onion

rosemary

1 Sift the flour and salt into a large mixing bowl. Stir in the yeast. Make a well in the centre of the dry ingredients. Pour in the water and 30 ml/2 tbsp of the oil. Mix well, adding a little more water if the mixture seems dry.

2 Knead the dough on a lightly floured surface for about 10 minutes until smooth and elastic.

3 Place the dough in a greased bowl, cover and leave in a warm place for about 1 hour until doubled in bulk. Knock back and knead the dough for 2–3 minutes.

4 Meanwhile, preheat the oven to 220°C/425°F/Gas 7. Roll out the dough to a large circle, about 1 cm/½ in thick, and transfer to a greased baking sheet. Brush with the remaining oil.

5 Halve the onion and slice into thin wedges. Sprinkle over the dough, with the rosemary and sea salt, pressing them in lightly.

6 Using a finger, make deep indentations in the dough. Cover the surface with clear film, then leave to rise in a warm place for 30 minutes. Remove the clear film and bake for 25–30 minutes until golden. Serve warm.

Saffron and Basil Breadsticks

Saffron lends its delicate aroma and flavour, as well as rich yellow colour, to these tasty breadsticks.

Makes 32

INGREDIENTS
generous pinch of saffron strands
30 ml/2 tbsp hot water
450 g/1 lb/4 cups strong white flour
5 ml/1 tsp salt
10 ml/2 tsp easy-blend dried yeast
300 ml/½ pint/1¼ cups lukewarm
    water
45 ml/3 tbsp olive oil
45 ml/3 tbsp chopped fresh basil

strong white flour

water

olive oil

saffron strands

basil

easy-blend yeast

salt

1 Put the saffron strands in a small heatproof bowl. Add the hot water and leave to soak for 10 minutes.

2 Sift the flour and salt into a large mixing bowl. Stir in the yeast, then make a well in the centre of the dry ingredients. Pour in the water and saffron liquid and start to mix a little.

3 Add the oil and basil and continue to mix to a soft dough.

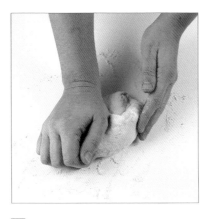

4 Knead the dough on a lightly floured surface for about 10 minutes until smooth and elastic. Place in a greased bowl, cover with clear film and leave for about 1 hour until it has doubled in bulk.

5 Knock back the dough, then transfer it to a lightly floured surface and knead for 2–3 minutes.

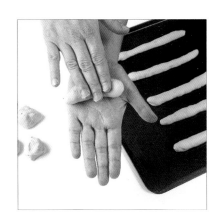

6 Preheat the oven to 220°C/425°F/ Gas 7. Divide the dough into 32 pieces and shape into long sticks. Place well apart on greased baking sheets, then leave for a further 15–30 minutes until they become puffy. Bake for about 15 minutes until crisp and golden. Serve warm.

INDEX

A

Artichoke salad, sweet and sour, 23
Asparagus with eggs, 71
Aubergines: aubergine, lemon and caper salad, 76
    penne with aubergine and mint pesto, 40
Avocado sauce, tagliatelle with, 38

B

Beans: spaghetti with mixed bean chilli sauce, 34
    Tuscan bean soup, 27
Béchamel sauce, 21
Breads, 90-4
Broccoli with garlic, 80

C

Cannelloni, vegetarian, 52-3
Capellini, lemon and Parmesan, 42
Carrots, marsala, 80
Cauliflower: creamy Parmesan and cauliflower soup, 28
    Gorgonzola, cauliflower and walnut gratin, 69
Cheese: pasta with Gorgonzola and walnut sauce, 44
    tortellini with three cheeses, 37
Chillies, 16
    chilli oil, 17
Conchiglie, spinach and ricotta, 46
Coriander ravioli with pumpkin filling, 48
Courgettes with sun-dried tomatoes, 70

D

Dolcelatte-stuffed pears, 24

E

Eggs: egg and cheese soup, 30
    potato and red pepper frittata, 67

F

Farfalle with mushrooms and cheese, 45
Fennel: baked fennel with Parmesan cheese, 72
    fennel, orange and rocket salad, 76
Focaccia, rosemary and sea salt, 92

G

Garden salad, 75
Garlic, 16
    garlic oil, 17
Gnocchi, spinach and ricotta, 66
Gorgonzola, cauliflower and walnut gratin, 69

H

Herbs, 16
    fresh herb pizza, 54

L

Lasagne, baked vegetable, 50
Leeks: leek, mushroom and lemon risotto, 60
    leek, potato and rocket soup, 31
Lemon ricotta cake, 84
Lovers' knots, 88

M

Marsala carrots, 80
Minestrone, 26
Mushrooms: farfalle with cheese and, 45
    leek, mushroom and lemon risotto, 60
    polenta with mushroom sauce, 64-5
    roast mushroom caps with parsley, 72
    spaghetti with mushroom and olive sauce, 35
    wild mushroom pizzettes, 58

O

Oils, 17
Olives, 17
Onions, 15

P

Pasta, 14, 19, 32-53
Pasta with Gorgonzola and walnut sauce, 44
Peaches with amaretti, 84
Pears, dolcelatte-stuffed, 24
Penne with aubergine and mint pesto, 40
Peppers: pepper gratin, 22
    stuffed peppers, 82
Pesto, 20
Pine nut tart, 86
Pizzas, 18, 54-9
Polenta with mushroom sauce, 64-5
Potatoes: new potato, rosemary and garlic pizza, 59
    potato and red pepper frittata, 67
    potatoes baked with tomatoes, 68
Pumpkin: coriander ravioli with pumpkin filling, 48
    pumpkin and pistachio risotto, 62-3

R

Radicchio pizza, 55
Ravioli, coriander with pumpkin filling, 48
Risotto, 60-3

S

Saffron and basil breadsticks, 94
Salads, 25, 75-9
Sauces, 20-1
Soups, 26-31
Spaghetti: with tomato sauce, 32
    with mixed bean chilli sauce, 34
    with mushroom and olive sauce, 35

Spinach: spinach and ricotta conchiglie, 46
    spinach and ricotta gnocchi, 66
Stock, vegetable, 19
Summer pasta salad, 78

T

Tagliatelle: with an avocado sauce, 38
    with double tomato sauce, 36
Tiramisu, 87
Tomatoes, 15
    easy tomato sauce, 20
    fresh tomato soup, 29
    spaghetti with tomato sauce, 32
    sun-dried tomato bread, 90
    tagliatelle with double tomato sauce, 36
Tortellini with three cheeses, 37
Tricolore pasta salad, 25
Tuscan bean soup, 27

V

Vegetables: baked vegetable lasagne, 50
    marinated vegetable antipasti, 74
    spring vegetable and pine nut pizza, 56
    vegetable stock, 19
Vegetarian cannelloni, 52-3

W

Walnut bread, 91
Wholemeal pasta, asparagus and potato salad, 79

Z

Zabaglione, 88